Catullus—The Complete Poetry

D1097209

Translated, with an Introduction, by Frank O. Copley

Gaius Valerius Catullus

The

Complete

Poetry

Ann Arbor Paperbacks
The University of Michigan Press

Second printing 1966
First edition as an Ann Arbor Paperback 1964
Copyright © by The University of Michigan 1957
Published in the United States of America by
The University of Michigan Press and simultaneously
in Toronto, Canada, by Ambassador Books Limited
Manufactured in the United States of America

Introduction

A lyric poem is itself. It tells us all that we need to
know about itself, or at least all that the poet wanted
us to know about it. If it springs from an occasion, the
occasion is there; if from a person, the person is
there. No one lyric poem depends on any other for its
worth or meaning; it is itself, a whole, an entity, a
complete unit of thought. We do not need to tie it
to something else in order to understand it. It is a
creature—a small creature, perhaps, but nonetheless
a creature. It speaks to you and it speaks to me. It
may say one thing to me and another to you, and
what it says to you or to me may be quite different
from what it said to its creator. It is read and valued
for the truth it has in itself. That truth is the truths
that its readers find in it.

To the understanding of a lyric poem, the biogra-
phy of its author is irrelevant. If this were not so, no
one would bother to read the poems of Gaius Valerius
Catullus, for we know virtually nothing of his life.
He was born at Verona; for this there is substantial
and reliable evidence. He was born in the middle
eighties, B.C., but whether the year was 87 or 86 or
85 or 84 we do not know. He died young, probably
in his early thirties. The poems themselves show

that he must have been alive in 55 B.C., and the probabilities are that he lived on to 54 or 53, or perhaps a few years later. There is only one date in his life that we can establish with certainty. In reading his poems we learn that he spent a year in the province of Bithynia on the staff of the governor, Memmius. Memmius was praetor in 58 B.C., and in accordance with usual practice ought to have been governor in the following year, 57. We have no proof that he was, but the assumption seems reasonably safe.

Of Catullus' family background we know a little. His father was a man of some wealth and prominence—at any rate, Julius Caesar made stopovers at his house on his passages between Gaul and Italy, and the Generalissimo (*imperator unicus*), as Catullus none too lovingly styled him, was not in the habit of imposing himself and his portentous retinue on nonentities. Catullus never mentions his father or any other member of his family except a brother, and he appears in the poems only after his death.

We do not know when Catullus left Verona and came to Rome, nor why he came nor how long he stayed there. He says once that Rome was his true home, but this was when he was away from there and was deeply unhappy. The sentiment may have been quite momentary. He seems to have circulated between Rome, Verona, a villa on Lake Garda (*Lacus Benacus*) and another near Tivoli (*Tibur*), but we do not know when he went to these places or why or how long he stayed or what he did there.

The poems that can be dated seem to fall in the years 57 to 54 B.C., but we cannot arrange the other poems around these datable ones in anything like a convincing chronology. Most of them could have been written at almost any time. Even the sizable group which centers around his love affair with the woman he calls Lesbia cannot be dated—not even around so obvious an incident as the Bithynia trip. (Did he meet and love her before or after the trip? Or did it come in the middle? There is no way to tell.) Scholars have amused themselves by arranging the Lesbia poems in such a way as to create a story of the affair, complete with first poem, last poem, quarrel(s), reconciliation(s), and the like. Speculation of this kind is intellectually diverting and may even turn up a fact or two, but it adds nothing to the meaning of the poems themselves and may even be misleading.

Much the same may be said of the persons whose names appear in the poems. Some are obvious: we can hardly miss Julius Caesar, Pompey, and Cicero. The slightly more experienced will spot Catullus' dear friend and constant associate, Gaius Licinius Calvus, lawyer and poet. The Cornelius of two poems is almost certainly Cornelius Nepos, historian and biographer; the Caelius of a number of others is probably Marcus Caelius Rufus, whom we know from Cicero's letters and the oration he delivered in his defense. We are reasonably confident, too, of Gaius Helvius Cinna, the poet—apparently the Charles Williams of his day, to judge from his interest in theology and the baffling complexity of his poems. Beyond this the doubt grows. Even Lesbia herself cannot be identified with certainty. Apuleius, writing nearly three hundred years later, says Lesbia's real name was Clodia, and no one has ever seriously questioned his statement. There was a Clodia in Rome in Catullus' day. Cicero knew her, and from his letters and speeches we gather that she was beautiful, brilliant, the center of a circle of political schemers and intellectuals, and totally devoid of principle of any kind. She had a husband somewhere in the house, a man named Metellus Celer, but he seems not to have bothered her much. She had a brother, Clodius, who was Cicero's political and personal enemy. Now Cicero was not above slanting the truth for political ends, so we may justly wonder if he may not have been a little hard on Clodius' fascinating sister; just the same, she was probably bad enough. She was some seven years older than Catullus. For many centuries now it has been generally assumed that she was Catullus' Lesbia. It is pleasant to think so, and does no harm.

The other persons whose names Catullus mentions are really just people he knew; they had best be left at that, if what we want to do is to read, enjoy, and understand his poems. Those who are curious as to what is known or guessed or conjectured about them may look in the introduction of almost any annotated edition of Catullus' poems (for example, that of E. T. Merrill, published now by Harvard University) for such information as there is. They will find each identification qualified by a "probably" or a "possibly." The fact is that the identity of these persons does not matter; the poems themselves tell us all that we need to know (and in a good many cases, all that we do know) about them. We do not need to know who Eliot's "Sweeney" is, or Cummings' "Goldberger." Catullus' "Aurelius" and "Manlius" and "Varus" are friends of theirs.

With mythological, historical, and geographical names the problem is not quite the same. Every poet assumes that his readers know things, not about himself but about the world he lives in, and sometimes he can be quite demanding. Eliot asks a lot. He expects us to know *The Tempest* and *Tristan* and Thomas à Becket, to mention only a few of the more obvious things. Cummings is a little less hard on us, but even he assumes that we know about Boston and Paris and Warren G. Harding. Eliot and Cummings are writing for the English-speaking world of the twentieth century A.D. Catullus wrote for the Latin-speaking world of the first century B.C. His readers knew about Diana and Troy and Cyrene and Hercules; they knew about omens and the evil eye and Venus and Cupid. Because our world is a Graeco-Roman world (with additaments and embellishments from other cultures) we know a good many of these things, too, and our position as Catullus' readers is not so difficult as might at first appear. And for that matter, the point of Catullus' references to such things is usually quite obvious even when the thing itself is unknown to us. Still it helps, occasionally, to know, and I have therefore appended a few notes to the poems when it seemed to me that the reader might find himself so far from Catullus' world as to be uncomfortable. For anything further, the curious are referred to any standard dictionary of classical antiquities (for example, the *Oxford Classical Dictionary*).

It may be interesting, although again it is not necessary, to know a little something about Catullus as a literary figure. The Romans of later ages almost always call him *doctus,* an epithet which scholars for many centuries have been uneasily rendering as "learned." Uneasily, that is, because although that is what *doctus* ought to mean, the appellation seems peculiarly inappropriate in Catullus' case. His poems are anything but "learned," at least as we understand the word. He was well educated and widely read, to be sure. He knew Greek literature from Homer on down to the works still being produced in the Greek world of his own day. He knew the earlier Latin writers, most of whom, except for Plautus and Terence, are hardly more than names to us now: Andronicus and Naevius and Ennius and Lucilius and Laevius, to mention only a few. But it is doubtful that he had read much more than any other cultivated man of his times. What he read was what everybody was reading. Scholars, noting his interest in poetic form, and his occasional ventures into the literary manner of the Greeks of Alexandria, have tied this up with the troublesome term, *doctus,* and with a few other bits of scholarly lore, to make out that he was an "Alexandrian," an imitator of the Greek scholar-poets who centered around the great library of the Ptolemies in the fourth and third centuries B.C. This would make a neat pigeonhole, if Catullus would only fit it. The trouble is that he is as much an "imitator" of Sappho and Archilochus and Homer as he is of the Alexandrians.

Actually, it is wrong to call him an "imitator" at all. All great poets learn from their predecessors, and Catullus did, too, but only a classical scholar would think of calling them "imitators" because of it. He is no more of an "imitator" than Keats or Byron or Dylan Thomas. If he was "learned," so are they. The fact is, we do not know how or why the epithet came to be attached to his name. Either we do not really know what *doctus* means, which is possible, or else the appellation is one of those literary accidents such as we have seen happen to poets of our own times, like Shakespeare's "native wood-notes wild" or Milton's "organ-tones." Somebody said it once; it sounded good, and people have been repeating it ever since.

What was Catullus? He was a rebel, a radical, an experimenter, an innovator, a pioneer. There were a lot of them in Rome then. It was a time of furious unrest, politically, socially, economically, and intellectually. The republic, honored and ancient but hopelessly clumsy, was falling apart. It could rule Latium; it could not rule the world. Cicero, devoted patriot, was trying to shore it up. Caesar went calmly about his business, waiting for the collapse to proceed far enough for him to move in with his new imperial ideas. Society was a wreck, with too many men having too much money, too much power, and too few principles. Marriage was something that had to be gone through to get a divorce. Public office and the courts were for sale. It was an immoral, dangerous, and fascinating age. Ideas were everywhere. Cicero was turning out volume after volume of his systematizations of Greek philosophy. Lucretius was writing his poem on Epicureanism. Gentlemen, well-read or not, skilled or unskilled, were manufacturing Latin versions of Greek tragedy and epic. Some, like Cicero again, were writing original poems. Literary endeavor of one sort or another was the mark of the educated man.

Since great poets are rare at any time, most of this must have been quite mediocre. Of these scribblings of Roman gentlemen, all that is left are some bits and scraps of Cicero's verse. It is skillful but stodgy and conventional. Trying to be lofty and noble, it is only pretentious and dull. A generation ago we would have called it Victorian. Earlier Roman poets, to judge from the extant fragments, had been original, imaginative, sensitive, and enthusiastic. Somewhere along the line their spirit had been lost.

However, even before Catullus' day there were signs of a regeneration. In the nineties, B.C., the poet Laevius made the first breech in the walls of conventionalism. His "Little Poems on Love" (*Erotopaegnia*), of which, unfortunately, only the barest fragments survive, introduced the Romans to the light occasional lyric, revivified the language of poetry by letting it speak the way people really spoke—a language full of colorful and imaginative metaphors, diminutives, Greek loan-words, gaiety, and humor. He showed that Latin could use with complete adequacy the bright and sparkling lyric metres of the Greeks. Like Gerard Manley Hopkins, he was a generation ahead of his time. He must have been regarded, like Hopkins, as a freak.

But the break had been made, and in the fifties and forties and on into the thirties B.C. a whole company of young poets began to experiment in new directions. Cicero, who naturally did not like them, calls them "Young Turks" (*Neoteroi*); Horace, who learned much of his own art from them, ungraciously calls them literary ancestor-worshippers (they had taken the grand old satirist, Lucilius, as their patron saint), vulgarians (they had a fondness for pungent metaphor), and cheap popularity-seekers (they thought that poetry might be made to say something to a lot of people). They wrote lyric, epigram, elegy, and even epic; they tried new metres and different styles, ranging all the way from the tenuously delicate to the horrendously bombastic. Perhaps in response to the decay of the state cult (another Roman institution that was falling apart from inadequacy) they developed an interest in theology, and particularly in the worship of Cybele, the Great Mother of the Gods. Whether there were among them converts to some kind of neo-orthodoxy, like Williams, Eliot, and Auden in our day, we cannot say, but the analogy is tempting. Their leader was Valerius Cato, teacher, scholar, and critic, whose critical judgment—at least so one of them says—was enough to make or break a poet. So little is left of what they wrote that we can pass no independent judgment on its worth. Such furious activity and endless experimenting must have produced some literary monstrosities, but it also produced the forms, the metres, the language, and above all, the literary freedom that incubated Horace, Vergil, Tibullus, Propertius, and Ovid.

Catullus was one of these young rebels. He is in fact the only one whose works have survived. The others we know only by what people like Cicero and Horace have to say about them, and by the occasional lines quoted from them by antiquarians like Aulus Gellius. And how representative of them is Catullus? Who knows? Horace sneeringly names him one of their leaders; at least that is what he appears to be doing, but the meaning of the passage in question is still being debated. None of his contemporaries except Cornelius Nepos even so much as mentions his name. If we have correctly understood Catullus' introductory poem (No. 1) it would seem that people in general classified his poems as "stuff" (*nugae*), and we may well suspect that they produced much the same effect on the reading public of his day that Cummings' *Tulips and Chimneys* produced in this country when it first appeared. A few people, like Nepos, had the patience and good will to read and study and understand; the rest thought it hardly worth the bother.

We do not really know, then, whether Catullus was a leader among the "Young Turks," whether his work may safely be regarded as representative of theirs, or whether he was just one of them and as different from the rest as they all were from refined poetasters like Cicero. Within a century they were all but forgotten; he survived to become a classic among the Roman poets, read and studied even by people who paid him no honor beyond that of profiting from his poetic pioneering and of stealing his lines. He continued to be read and quoted and learned from (I will not say "imitated") well into the fifth century A.D. Then, by some accident, he was lost, but since his rediscovery in the fourteenth century he has never been forgotten.

I have said that he was a radical and a pioneer. To the modern reader his poems will probably seem neither radical nor pioneering. We are used to the kind of poetry he writes. But we must remember that

Catullus himself is at least part of the reason why we are used to it. He, and of course the other "Young Turks," whom it would be unfair to forget, released Latin poetry from an exclusive devotion to war, history, mythology, and astronomy. He dared take seriously subjects that up to then had been considered fit only for the doggerel of the dinner table or the tavern: love and wine and friends and enemies and the hundred happenings of the day. He saw the cogency and power in the ordinary spoken language of Italy; his poems for the most part have all the ease and simplicity, the clarity and the subtlety of a conversation between good friends. But he also understood the poetry of slang and obscenity; he knew that even the polite formula and the dull cliché had their poetic uses. In the right spots, he saw, even stiff and unnatural artificiality, fulsome repetitiousness, and nonfunctional ornamentation could be employed to good effect. In metrics he was smooth and precise, or rough and clumsy, in ever sensitive response to the demands of the task in hand—and sometimes perhaps in response to a puckish desire to see what would happen. Few poets have understood as well as he the scope of the lyric; very few have responded to its demands with such sensitivity and with a taste so nearly infallible. No doubt he made mistakes; certainly he did things with metre, style, and vocabulary that no other Roman cared, or dared, to imitate. In the end, he was one of the poets who made it possible for the lyric to be what it is today.

Catullus—The Complete Poetry

one

who'll I dedicate my pretty new book to
all fresh and
        shiny and
                just off the shelf?
Cornelius, to you: you always thought
the stuff I wrote (that's what they called it—
        stuff)
was not so bad, not so bad
yes, and that was even when you had the nerve
        (that's what they called it—
        nerve)
to write the Outline of History
        in three
                short volumes
the LEARNING that went into them (Jupiter!)
the WORK!
well anyway, here
        take it
maybe it's not so much
maybe it's not so good

but just the same
       O Patron Maid
let it last forever
       not just for This
generation.

two

little bird, her darling
    (sometimes when she plays with you
    she suddenly holds you tight to her breast
    or sticks out a finger—oo, you little rascal
    you peck, go on do it again, harder, oo
    that's when my (how I wish I were with her
        she's so beautiful
    feels preciously a little gay
    (longing perhaps she thinks of me
    and this helps make it easier to bear
        as when passion heavy flames
        and then, dies, down
    I'd like to play with you the way she does
    and soothe within my heart the ache of love

two b

I like it as much as they say
that girl quick-footed liked
the little old golden apple
that untied the sash
she'd kept fastened so long

three

weep, Venus; Cupid, weep
weep everyone who loves nice things
the little bird is dead, her bird,
the little bird, the darling, hers
she loved it more than anything else in the world
it was a sweet little thing
why it knew her—they were maid and mother, like.
it used to stay on her lap, never tried to get away
it hopped around (there it goes! no, it's going over this way!)
she was its mistress, it sang for her
and not ever for anybody else.
now it's going along the dark, scary road
down there
and nobody comes back from there, they say.
well, damn you anyway, damned night of hell
anything that's pretty you just have to gulp it down,
don't you?

such a pretty little bird
just had to grab it, didn't you?
it's just too damned bad.
O birdie, birdie, birdie, see what you've done
to her
she's crying, they're all swollen and red
her lovely eyes.

four

my boat there
          (see her, friends)
she says she was the fastest of them all
show her anything that floats
          Speed?
you couldn't have stopped her from passing it
you want oars? you want sails?
whichever you liked, she really FLEW
and on that point she says you'll get no argument
from the shores of the Adriatic
          (scared the hell out of us, the Adriatic)
no nor from the Isles of Greece
or Rhodes (you all know Rhodes)
or the Propontis (just off Thrace, choppy and I mean
     CHOPPY)
or the Black Sea (a real stinker, that one)
(that's where she came from, you know;
they made a boat out of her, but before that
she was just woods

ever hear of Mount Cytorus?
that's where she stood
and talked and whispered when the wind
blew in her hair)
Amastris, Black Sea town,
Mount Cytorus, where the boxwood grows,
you knew all this, you know it now
perfectly well,
so says my boat.
when she first began to be
on you she stood, up near the top
in your water she first wet her oars
that's where she started from, and then
through sea after sea, stormy all,
she carried her owner whether she took the breeze
on port or starboard quarter or when Jupiter
decided he liked us came 'round right astern
and gave a good yank to both sheets at once.
she didn't have to waste breath making prayers
to the reef-gods
not one single prayer
from the day she left that sea so far off there
all the way up to this calm little lake.
well that's all over now
she's laid up
she's getting old
she's taking her well-earned rest
she's making herself an offering to you,
Twin Castor and Castor's Twin.

five

I said to her, darling, I said
let's LIVE and
let's LOVE and
what do we care what those old
purveyors of joylessness say?
(they can go to hell, all of them)
the Sun dies every night
in the morning he's there again
you and I, now,
when our briefly tiny light flicks out,
it's night for us, one single
everlasting
Night.
give me a kiss, a hundred a thousand kisses,
a fifty eleven seven hundred thousand
kisses, and let's
do it all over again
        Darling
how many, how many, you say?
mix them up; it's bad luck
to know how many; wouldn't want people
to count, them, up
somebody might have the Evil Eye
and if he knew he just might
BEWITCH
them.

six

Flavius' got a gal and I bet she's a honey
who is she, huh? c'mon, tell Catullus
     y' aren't gonna tell?
pretty bad, must be, 'cause if she wasn't
     (talk about telling)
     ya couldn't keep yer mouth shut
ya got yerself a flooz
     hot like a fever
     (fever-flooz, fever-flooz
        boy, you can have 'er!)
that's why y' aren't telling, can't fool me
you aren't sleeping alone these nights
yer bed can't talk, but (boy!) it don't need to
smells like rosebuds and (whew!) what perfume
and look at them pillows, both messed up
and look at that bedstead all shook to pieces
the damn thing squeaks and prac'ly does the shimmy
you been doin' it, ya might as well admit it
how d' I know? say, ya don't look like you do
if ya ain't been up to some monkey-business
c'mon now, Flav (what's the odds?) c'mon let's have it
     I wanta write a pome
     about you and yer gal
       and set you both
         on the HEIGHTS OF HEAVEN

seven

Darling
you want to know
how many times you've got to kiss me
before I'll have enough and to suit?
       what's the number of the sands
       in sylphium-land Cyrene lie
       starting where Jove's hot temple stands
       up to Old Battus' holy tomb
or
       how many stars when silent hangs
       the night
       look down and see
       men filching love
just kiss me kisses that many times
("crazy!")
all right, crazy, but that's what'll suit
       Catullus
just so the buzzy busy people
can't count, them, up
and no gabble tongue
can put the hex on them.

eight

Catullus, it's too bad, but don't be silly
you see it's gone; well, gone is gone, that's all
the sunshine in those days was bright to you
when you but followed where the Girl led on
beloved of me as none shall ever be loved
we laughed so much then doing those many things
which you wanted—and when did the Girl say no?
the sunshine then was truly bright to you
now she says no; you idiot, say no, too,
don't chase a runaway; don't get all down,
lock up your heart! stand it! and don't give in!
goodbye my Girl! Catullus will not give in
he'll not run after you; he'll do no begging
but you'll be sorry when nobody begs you.
she-devil, damn you! what life's left for you?
who'll come your way? who'll say "now there's a beauty?"
whom will you find to love? who'll call you his?
whom will you kiss? in whose lips set your teeth?
stop, Catullus! it's over: don't give in.

nine

Veranius out of all number friend
(three thousand or more they say they are)
in heart the one you only the truly one,

home? are you home and said you hail
to household gods, to brothers one of mind
and to your grey-haired mother, too?
you are! this joyfully I hear
I'll see you (not a scratch, you're all of you)
I'll hear you (Spain it was, I think)
telling the tale of what I saw
       ("that reminds me of the time—was it in Cordova
       or Cadiz?
       and that night
       but the best was when
       you meet the queerest—I remember one")
for I know, your, way.
your hand my hand, my shoulder shoulder of you
in touch of You and Me and warmly grasp,
O all the gladness in a world of glad
where happier gladder is one thing than me?

ten

you know Varus don't you
      (friend of mine)
he's got a girl, see, and he took me to meet her
      (I was downtown with time hanging on my hands)
Some Little Floozy
      thinks I when I first lay eyes on her
yeah y'know kinda cute and nice at that
well we go along
talking about all kindsa things

and then right in the middle they ask me
how's Bithynia
what sorta place is it
make any money out there?
I tell 'em the truth, see
there's nothing there
the people got nothing
the brass got nothing
the staff's got nothing
nobody gets any cumshaw outa that place
especially if you gotta sonovabitch
for a boss, don't give a damn for his men
yeah but even so, they say
the specialty of the place
you bought that, didn't you—
litter-bearers?
well I wanted the girl to think
I was maybe a little better off than the others
so I says Oh after all
I wasn't quite so down on my luck
that just because I drew a lousy territory
I couldn't buy eight husky boys
(boys? I hadn't one boy either here or there
who could pick up the busted pole of an old stretcher
and put it on his shoulder)
here she says (you mighta known she would
        the little bitch)
aw please she says Catullus just a little while
lend me your boys—I'd kinda like to ride
down to Sarapis' temple
now waitaminit I says to the gal
I guess I did say they were mine, didn't I
well I got kinda mixed up

you know my friend Cinna
      Gaius Cinna
he was the one bought them
but maybe they're his maybe they're mine
it don't matter, does it
I use them all the time just like if I'd bought them

awright go on and laugh; you make me tired
you're around, a guy don't dare make a little slip

eleven

Furius and Aurelius!
you'll follow faithful in Catullus' way
if he shall pierce to India's utmost lands
that shore afar where echoing in the East
      the surf is pounding

or to Hyrcania, Araby the Blest,
to Sacia, Parthia, where men bear the bow,
or to those seas which with its seven mouths
      the Nile discolors

or if across the Alps he'll turn his tread
to see where Caesar went, and know him great—
the Gaulish Rhine, the fearsome sea, and last,
      the land of Britain

all this, oh yes, whatever heaven's will
shall bring, you stand prepared to try with him—
take to that girl of mine a message brief,
      brief, and not kindly

to her and her kept lovers, a fond farewell,
those hundreds whom she holds in one embrace
she loves not one, but bursts—again, again!—
      their swollen passion.

she'll find no more a haven in my love,
for by her fault it fell, as on the lea's
last edge and end a flower, when the plow
      passed by and touched it.

twelve

my friend, watch that left hand of yours
I don't think much of what you do with it
when we're all laughing and the wine goes 'round
that nowyouseeit nowyoudon't business
with people's napkins if they don't tie 'em down
funny, huh? not so you could notice it,
      my corny pal
it's as unwitty and unlovely as they come
don't think so? well, your brother does
he'd give a million to stop your pinching stuff
he knows what's funny and what isn't, and his taste
      isn't all in his mouth

I'm telling you now, watch out
I've got three hundred verses ready
          to fire your way
if you don't send back my napkin
yes, I know it isn't worth a lot
          that's not what's bothering me
but it's a present from a friend of mine
it's Spanish stuff, see, came from Taragon,
a gift to me from Fabullus
          (and Veranius too, I guess)
how do you think I feel about it
when I feel the way I do
about Veranius (dear old V)
          and
                    Fabullus?

thirteen

say Fabullus
you'll get a swell dinner at my house
a couple three days from now (if your luck holds out)
all you gotta do is bring the dinner
          and make it good and be sure there's plenty
Oh yes don't forget a girl (I like blondes)
and a bottle a wine maybe
          and any good jokes and stories you've heard
you just do that like I tell you ol' pal ol' pal
you'll get a swell dinner
          ?
          what,

about,
ME?

well;

well here take a look in my wallet,
yeah those're cobwebs

but here,

I'll give you something too
I CAN'T GIVE YOU ANYTHING BUT
LOVE BABY

no?
well here's something nicer and a little more cherce maybe
I got a perfume see
it was a gift to HER
straight from VENUS and CUPID LTD.
when you get a whiff of that you'll pray the gods
to make you (yes you will, Fabullus)
ALL
NOSE

fourteen

my dear, dear Calvus
it's a good thing for you
that I consider you
the best friend I've got
because if I didn't
after what you sent me
I wouldn't be able to stand

the sight of you
what did I do,
what did I say,
why you had to ruin me
          wit all dem
                    poits
musta been some (I hope he chokes)
client of yours
sent you such a heap of junk
but wait, say, it wasn't that (was it?) professor guy
that's giving them—o quaite new veddy choice—
if it was I don't feel quite so sick
in fact I'm happy, tickled pink
that all your work isn't going
down the well-known drain

judas priest, wotta godawful Kollectit Pomes
and you sent them to, you call me your, friend
watcha tryna do, kill me or sumpin?
and on the Saturnalia, too, nicest day in the year
oh no, uh-uh, smartypants, just you wait
if morning ever comes
I'm goin to the bookstore, the bookstore, the bookstore,
I'm gonna buy some poitry, some poitry, some poitry,
some nice, poison poitry
and send it all to Calvus, with love,
          (that'll teach you)

good lord, that book's still here
good-bye! get out!

take your love-dove moon-june
back where it came from
P
U
you
stink

fourteen b

if
just possibly
maybe
perhaps
someday
some of you people
will take the trouble
to read what I wrote
          (flapdoodle, is it?)
and don't think
it'll curl
your hair
to lay your
lily-whites
on
me. . . . . .

fifteen

compliments to you
from me and my dear boy,
Aurelius, I'd like to make one humble request
to-wit and namely:
was there anything ever
you sort of wanted to maybe keep
kind of decent and clean like? if so
keep an eye on the kid for me, will you
you know, keep him out of trouble
I don't mean from people in general
I'm not worried about the folks you see
in the street going up and down
with their minds on their own beeswax
no, it's you I'm worried about and that Tendency of yours
bodes no good for any kid no matter who
follow your inclinations any place, any time,
as much as you like so long as it's somewhere else
this one kid I'd like to make an exception of
          if you don't think it's too damned much to ask.
but if your dirty mind and brainless brash
cause you to make so serious a mistake
as to lay booby-traps to blow up in my face
you'll be sorry, you'll wish you hadn't
they'll haul you to the front door
they'll lay you out
and give you the Treatment
reserved for guys like you

sixteen

nuts to you, boys, nuts and go to hell
you pair of little snots, you lacypants
            Aurelius
                and
            Furius
you read my verses, found a D---y W--d
(good gracious deary me!) and came to the
proFOUND conCLUsion
that I was just a dirty devil too
NOW LOOK
a poet's supposed to have some sense
of decency and taste
but nobody ever said his poems
had to be censored by the Purity League
            they'd have no fun
            they'd have no sparkle
without a dash of the age-old itch
and something to rouse the Ancient Urge
            (and I don't mean just for you young birds
            but for those old boys who've kinda lost
                    the swing of things)

but you
you read about a thousand kisses or so
and want to make a fairy out of me?
nuts to you, boys, nuts and go to hell

seventeen

Colonia
OCO
LOH
nee
yah
you gotta bridge, a nice Long Bridge
an ya wanna havva dance
on yer nice long bridge, but,
How ya Gonna Dance
          (yeh, howyagonna dance)
on a Bridge Like That
          (yeh, a bridge like that)
ya musta robbed a junk-yard
to git them planks
          (it'll fall on its face an go sleepy-bye
          out in the middle where they never found no bottom)
Well(!) Now(!)
Look(!)
howja like a Good bridge
a really truly dream-bridge
where yer whole town could do a
          Jump Jim Crow

you can have my wishes for it, all my best wishes for it
if you'll do just one thing for me.
all I want, Colonia, is a big laugh
just a fine fat juicy fat big fat belly-laugh:
you gotta man lives in your town
          (you and I know him: you'll see who I mean)

take him out and throw him head-first from your bridge
      head down, foot down, straight in the mud down
(but pick out the place in that stinking swamp
where the guck is the bluest and blackest and the deepest)
the guy is a dope just a
big, plain, dope
ain't got the sense of a two-year-old kid
      goin' rock-a-bye-baby on papa's arm
he's got a wife what a greeny bloomy gal
what a jumpy little frisky little honey of a gal
what a watch-me-buddy-I-bruise-easy luscious kind of gal
she wanders where she wants to: he don't give a damn
just sits there lies
there like a lumpa
lead there
sees about as much as if she wasn't there at all
that's Mr. Dope-schmope
eyes no
ears no
alive no dead no
don't know which it is.
take him out and belly-flop him
right from yer bridge
might wake Drowsy-frowzy out of his dream
might leave his dull soul down in the muck
like a mule leaves a shoe behind
caught in sticky guck.

twenty-one

Aurelius great grandaddy of all
hungers
        (not just those you see, but
        all there ever were or are or
        shall be now and forever more)
you want to get next to my little friend
and y' aren't subtle about it either you hang
        around you kid
        him along you stick
        to him like glue you try just
        about
        Everything
you won't get away with it; lay me
any traps you want I'll lay you
first
and know what, if you were flush
I wouldn't have a word to say
but what gets me down, the kid's
learning from you to like being hungry
and thirsty, so I tell you now
while the quitting's good
quit layin' or you'll quit
laid

twenty-two

Varus
you take Suffenus now (you know
him right enough) he's a nice
fellow and he always has
something to say that's fun
but then again he beats us all
at turning the verses out
I bet he's got ten thousand
maybe more all finished off
and not (you know) the way we do
put down on any handy scrap around
no, sir! it's royal bond, brand-new,
new bosses, purple thongs, and sheepskin
ruled with lead, and pumice
to polish the whole job off
just read the stuff and that nice guy
that seemed such fun, Suffenus, sounds
like he oughta be milkin' a goat
or diggin' a ditch, you'd think he'd scare
himself, God, what a change!
now what do you make of that? he looked as smooth
a minute ago as anything
you ever heard of or even more
but flatter he falls than the flat Flatlands
the minute he takes to poetry
and what beats all, he's never so gay
as when he's writing a poem, he's such a joy
to himself he can hardly believe
he's as good as that. well, now of course

we all make the same mistake, show me the man
who isn't just like Suffenus in some way
we've got our blind spots, every one,
but we just never see what hangs behind.

twenty-three

Furius has no slave, no bank-account
no bed-bug and no spider and no fire
but he has a father and a step-mother
who've got the teeth to chew flint and spit sand
        you get along fine, your father and you
        and that hardwood hussy he calls a wife
that's no surprise; you all enjoy good health
got fine digestion, not one thing to fear:
no house to burn or fall around your ears,
nothing to steal, no poison in your drink,
no risk of loss of any kind at all.
        you've built up bodies sound as a nut
        (or anything else that's sounder than that)
        living on crusts in the sun and the rain.
why shouldn't you have the Good and Happy Life?
        you never sweat, you never spit,
        no phlegm in your throat, no runny nose
        and—special note of purity—
        you're clean as a whistle there behind
        and as for committing nuisances
        you do that not ten times a year
        o dainty bean! o pebble pure!
        you never need to wash your hands!

Furius, you've got that Rich and Happy Life!
don't toss it aside! don't value it so low!
that hundred thousand you keep begging for
forget it, friend! why, you're a Happy Man!

twenty-four

O flowret of all the Juventiuses
not only those that are but those that were
or shall hereafter be in other years,
I'd rather you'd give the gold of Midas
to that man who has no slave nor bank-account
than let yourself be loved by him like that.
"why? isn't he nice enough" you say? he is,
he's nice, but has no slave nor bank-account.
make light of it, excuse it as you please,
fact is, he has no slave nor bank-account.

twenty-five

Dear Thallus, you're a fairy; you're softer than bunny-fur
or fuzzy-wuzzy eiderdown or lobe of a dear little ear
or languid loins of a tired old man where the spider spins his
    web;

but Thallus, you're more grabby than a gust of the wild wild-
    wind
when a lady divine . . . .
. . . . and there they sit and yawn
. . . .
send back my coat—oh, yes, it's mine!—I mean the one you
    stole,
my Spanish napkin, too, and my Bithynian writing-pad
(did you have to show them all around and say they were
    Grandpa's own?)
now just unglue them from your claws and send them back
    to me,
or that fanny white as a little lamb and those softy pinky-paws
will get all scribbled up with red where my whip has made its
    mark,
and you will dance as never before, like a little bit of a boat
caught out on the open ocean by a banshee blast of wind.

twenty-six

Furius, that little place of yours
was it the South Wind's blast and draft
you put it up against? the West Wind's, maybe?
the North?
the East?
oh—it was Fifteen Thousand and Two Hundred!
awful, deadly blow
(wind and crack your checks)

twenty-seven

good old Falerno, boy, that's what I want
splash it in my cup and make it good and strong
Postumia's passed her law, those are her orders
our lady drunker than the drunken grape.
water, get out, go anywhere but here
(spoil good wine!) some people take life hard
move in on them; mine will be Bacchus clear.

twenty-eight

Piso's pals, not a penny in your pockets,
bags all packed up and ready for departure,
good old Veranius dear old Fabullus
how're things? had enough? did that dirty devil
fill up your books with shivering and starving?
you have to write your profits in red ink, too?
just like me: I went out there with my praotor,
got one lone entry written down for profit:
            "Memmius, you stretched me out
            and fixed me up all nice and neat
            and then backed up and took your time
            and really let me have it."
from where I sit looks like you fared no better
you two got just as big a dose as I did.
that's what we get for suckin' round the blue-bloods.

Piso, Memmius, God and Goddess damn you,
you two blots on our country's fair escutcheon.

twenty-nine

who is there that can look at this, who is there that can stand
    it
(he'd have to have no sense of shame, propriety, or fairness)
Mamurra's got his hands on everything the long-haired Gauls
had called their own, and everything the Britons at world's
    end!
(you slimy son of Romulus, you know this and you stand it?)
and now he'll come with swollen head and pockets overflow-
    ing
and have himself a little tour through all the beds in town,
our little dovey lover-boy, our latter-day Adonis!
(you slimy son of Romulus, you know this and you stand it?
I see you have no sense of shame, propriety, or fairness!)
and was it all on this account, dear Generalissimo,
that you went off and spent your time on that far western isle
just so that worthless worn-out tool, your darling Dickie-boy,
could stuff his bank account with millions two—or was it
    three?
what's this, if it is not perverted generosity?
hadn't he thrown it around enough or squandered enough
    substance?
he took his father's money first and made a hash of that,
next, all he grafted from the war in Pontus; number three,

his Spanish gains (how well you know that tale, O golden
    Tagus!)
and now the Britons and the Gauls are trembling in their
    boots.
why do you nurse this dirty devil? pray, what can he do
except grab fine fat fortunes and go flush them down the
    drain?
was it for this, you heroes twain, our city's noblest souls,
father and son-in-law, that you have laid our country low?

thirty

Alfenus, you forgot; you were false to the friends that loved
    you.
have you no pity now, hard heart, for your dear old comrade?
can you betray me now, and lie and deceive me so blithely?
men can do wrong and lie, but God doesn't love them for it.
that's nothing to you, I gather. Oh, how you've left me to
    suffer!
tell me, what can men do? Of whom do they dare be trustful?
you were the one who bade me entrust my heart to your
    handling,
you led me into love, alleging that all was in safety
now you turn and back out, and all that you did and told me
you let the winds make vain, let ride with the clouds of
    heaven.
perhaps you forgot—but God remembers, Faith will remem-
    ber,

you will be sorry some later day for the wrong you have done
   me.

thirty-one

of Sirmio I sing
land of all headlands and islands
best and dearest
       (and Neptune bears them by the thousands
       in clear lakes bright and in the endless sea)
I'm glad I'm happy to be here
or am I here, I did
leave Thynia, didn't I, and Bithynia
       hotly dank flat
I see you, yes, I see you; safe, I'm home
o blessed peace when cares unshackled lie
o blessed rest when heart's of burden free
tired of foreign lands of travel tired
home have I come and on the very bed
I dreaming longed for soft to sleep I fall
this is it. now mark it paid in full
       for all my weary works and days
hello to you, dear Sirmio, I hope
you're half as glad to see me
I hope you're glad, too, waves of the lake I love
laugh out, shine out with smiles
home home again

thirty-two

please, Ipsithilla
my darling, my delight
tell me you'll be home
when I come in the hotly still of noon
tell me and if you tell
be this much kind to me
no lock to block the door
no note "gone out back soon"
stay home and make you ready for me
nine times to feel the pulse of love.
      what? you'll be busy?
      then tell me now
for I lie full and flat, and feel
love knocking, beating at my passion's door.

thirty-three

stick around the baths
and you'll see them operate
      king of thieves, Vibennius *père*
      princess of the May, Vibennius *fils*
      (what sticky fingers you've got, papa
      what an eager back you've got, sonny)
why not get out and go to hell
you two? V *père*'s a crook

and everybody knows it
and as for that ugly hump of yours
mon fils you'll find no takers
at a nickel a throw

thirty-four

hail Diana* we are thy loyal children
maids are we* and boys untouched of love
hail Diana* boys untouched of love
and maids* let our song rise to thee
thou art the daughter of Leto* and Jove the
          Almighty was thy Sire
thou art their mighty child* which thy Mother
          near the olive tree of Delos did lay down
lady of mountains thou wert to be* and of the
          greening woodlands
and of the leas that no man knows* and of the
          rivers roaring
thou art Lucina Juno when our mothers in the
          agony of childbirth* cry aloud unto thee
thou art the Power of Crossroads, Trivia* and for
          thy bastard light we call thee Moon
thou goddess with thy monthly course* dost measure
          the mileage of the year
and where in the fields the farmers' houses stand* thou
          fillest them with good things
in that Name whatsoever it pleaseth thee to be called*
          be thou Holy

and to us the people of Romulus as in time of old thou
       wert ever wont* grant the blessing of thy
       saving goodness.

thirty-five

My dear, young poet:
(he's a friend of mine, Caecilius by name,
and, little note, I wish you'd tell him, come
to Verona, please, and leave the new-built walls
of Comum, and the shore of Larius.
there is a thought or two I'd like to have
him hear—some ideas of his friend and mine.
so, if he's wise, he'll just burn up the road
for all that some fair maid may call him back
a thousand times when he starts out, and throw
both arms around his neck, and cry "No, wait!"
there *is* a girl, and if I'm told the truth
she's mad about him, just plain wild with love.
for she once read his poem—unfinished yet—
"Our Lady of Dindymus," and from then on
the poor thing's heart has been consumed by fire.
my dear, you're pardoned! your instinct for verse
is keen as Sappho's, for it's charming, quite,
Caecilius' "Lady,"—but unfinished still.)

thirty-six

you "Annals," by Volusius (god, what crap!)
come pay a votive offering for my girl.
for to the holy pair, Venus and Cupid
she promised that if I'd come back to her
and stop my vicious fusillade of verse
she'd take the "worst of poets'" choicest works
and give them to the limping-footed god
to burn upon some altar of bad cess.
and now that "worst of girls" sees that her vow
was just in fun, to give the gods a laugh.
and so—
       O thou born of the deep blue sea
       who dwellest in holy Idalium
       and Urii (that wretched port),
       Ancon, and Cnidus, Point-of-Reeds,
       and Amathus, and Golgi, too,
       not forgetting Dyrrhachium
       (that flophouse of the Upper Sea),
       please mark her vow as paid in full
       if it's been worth a laugh or two.
but you! step up now! hop right in the fire,
reeking of barnyards and of hayseed wit,
you "Annals," by Volusius (god, what crap!)

thirty-seven

you dirty cathouse and you its denizens
nine pillars down from the Boys with the liberty-caps
you think nobody's got the Power but you?
you think nobody else has got a right
to love the gals—the rest of us are all a bunch
of stinking goats?
just because you sit there in a line
with your fingers up your noses—a hundred
or two hundred of you—you think I wouldn't dare
to take the whole two hundred of you on?
go ahead and think so! I've got a lot
of dirty verse about you all and I'm gonna
scribble it all over the door
of your dirty cathouse
for there was a girl ran out on me
(beloved was she as none shall ever be loved)
a girl I put up many a battle for
she's taken up residence in that place of yours
she's the one you noble gentlemen
are making love to and (this is what makes it worst)
you're a bunch of pee-wees and back-alley whoresmen.
and you're the worst of all those lacy-pants
you son of the Celtiberian bunny-land,
Egnatius, whose only claim to fame
is your blue chin and your fine white teeth
scrubbed every night with Spanish P

thirty-eight

Cornificius!
sick at heart is Catullus, your dear friend,
sick at a heart that labors to beat on,
and worse and worse with every day and hour.
yet you—so easy and so small a thing—
what word of consolation have you sent?
I'm getting angry with you. Thus my love?
a little something, please, a word or two
more full of tears than old Simonides.

thirty-nine

that man Egnatius
somebody told him once he had fine white teeth
so now he smiles and smiles and smiles
suppose some poor devil's been hauled into court
his lawyer's even got the judge in tears
Egnatius smiles and smiles
let's say they're burying somebody's son
("such a nice boy, so good to his parents")
people are crying ("that's his mother—her only son—isn't it
    too bad?")
Egnatius smiles and smiles
no matter what's up, wherever he is, whatever's the deal,
he smiles and smiles. it's a disease he's got

and it isn't pretty, if you ask me, or funny, either.
it's no use, Egnatius m'boy; I've got to warn you:
if you were Roman or Sabine or Tiburtine
or a pinch-penny Umbrian or fat old Etruscan
or a horse-toothed greaser from Lanuvium
or a Transpadane (to toss my own folks in)
or anyone else that's clean about washing his teeth
I'd still say you oughtn't to smile and smile and smile
for there's nothing duller than a pointless smile
as it is, you're Spanish: in the land of Spain
they take the water that they make and every day
they scrub their teeth and rosy gums with it
and so:

> the higher the shine upon your teeth we see
> the more we know that you have drunk of P

forty

Say
what in the world's got into you
> you poor damn fool, Ravidus
what's the big idea
> running yourself head on into my verses?
are you sure you been saying your prayers right?
because I mean it's plain crazy stirring up a hassle
> with ME.
you looking for headlines?
are you sure you want . . . . . . kinda expensive this way,
> aren't they?

well o.k. you asked for it:
    you swiped my boy
    all right my friend
        I've only this to say
    go on have fun
    because my friend
        you'll pay
           and Pay
                and
    PAY

forty-one

Ameana
worn out whore
know what she wanted
a whole sawbuck
(yeah that's the one
    with the ugly snoot
    shacked up with that chiseler
    Dickie-boy from Formiae
she got any uncles or cousins or anything
    supposed to look out for her?
they better call in her friends
    and send for the medics
that gal's screwy
how long's it been
since she took a look
in her mirror?

forty-two

help, verses, help!
come a-running all of you
everywhere, all of you!
she thinks I'm a joke, that dirty tramp
and says she's not going to give me back
my writing-pad—if you can stand that!
let's get after her and lay it on the line—
you ask which one she is? there she goes—see her?—
with the ugly duck-waddle and the burlicue smirk,
got a grin on her face like the Hound of Gaul
get around her now and lay it on the line:
>   "dirty tramp, give me back my writing-pad
>   give me back my writing-pad, dirty tramp!
>   you don't give a hoot?
>   why you whorehouse muck
>   or anything else that's filthier than that . . ."
Huh? looks like even this won't be enough
well, if it's gotta be, we'll try a little force
we'll make that iron-bound bitch-face blush
shout it out again and shout it good and loud:
>   "dirty tramp, give me back my writing-pad
>   give me back my writing-pad, dirty tramp!"
Hey! we're getting nowhere, she's not a bit disturbed
looks like we gotta change our system and our plan
if you and I are going to make a dent in her:
>   "dear Lady, virtuous virgin pure
>   may I please have my writing-pad?"

forty-three

Hi there, sweetheart!
that nose of yours is not too small
your feet—well, hardly pretty
your eyes—well, hardly snappy
your fingers—not too long
your lips—you wiped your mouth yet?
your tongue—well, shall we say
         not the most elegant
aren't you Dickie-boy's girl—that chiseler from Formiae?
you mean to say that out in the sticks
they call you pretty?
you mean to say they've been comparing you
to Lesbia—my Lesbia?
O what a tasteless witless age!

forty-four

say, little summer-place
are you Sabine or Tiburtine?
because people who haven't got the heart
to hurt Catullus declare that you're Tiburtine
but those who've got the heart will bet
anything you like that you're just plain old Sabine
but whether you're Sabine or (more rightly) Tiburtine
I was glad to be at your little cottage

where I knocked a dreadful cough out of my chest.
I had it coming, got it from my stomach
(that's right!) when I succumbed to a passion
    for fancy banquets.
I wanted to go to Sestius' house for dinner—
you know that speech he made against Antius
during the last campaign—
      "you poison of the commonwealth
      you focus of infection in the state"
full of that sort of thing? I read it.
what happened? I caught the flu
and shivered and coughed myself to pieces
until I finally went into hiding
in your sheltering arms.
there I stayed in bed and lived on greens
until I got well.
I'm fine now, and you have my heartfelt thanks
because you refrained from taking that chance
to punish me for my sin
I'll never ask you to be so indulgent again
no, sir! if ever once more I so much as touch
the products of Sestius' poison pen
I pray that that icy stuff may bring a cold and a cough—
to me? no, not to me: to Sestius
that man who invites me to dinner
after—note: after!—I've read his dreadful speech.

forty-five

sweet Acme is Septimius' own true love
holding her close he says, "O Acme mine
if I don't love you madly, and to love
am not prepared, forever, all my years,
as much as he who can most madly love
alone in Libya or sun-baked India
may I the lynx-eyed lion run to meet."
        he spoke, and Love upon the left as first
          upon the right his approbation sneezed.
but Acme lightly bending back her head
to look into her loved lad's drunken eyes
kissed them with those encarmined lips of hers
and said, "So, light of my life, Septimius,
may we this lord alone forever serve
as a far greater and far fiercer flame
burns in the inner softness of my heart."
        she spoke, and Love upon the left as first
          upon the right his approbation sneezed.
now from an omen good they take their start
each has the other's heart for love to love

for Acme, Acme alone Septimius yearns
more than for Syria's and for Britain's wealth

for Septimius only Acme ever true
creates the joys delicious of her love.

what man has ever seen a richer pair
what man a Venus more disposed to bless?

forty-six

it's spring
warmly across the frozen world she came
(mad skies roared at the equinox
but Zephyr gently breathed them still)
Catullus, leave the Phrygian plains behind
and the green hothouse of Nicaea's farms
let's go to the Levant and see
the famous cities there
my heart trembles: how long? how many days?
my toes are dancing gay
goodbye, dear friends
sweet company of this year
how far from home together now we go
and scatter east west north and south
but every road we take
leads back to Rome.

forty-seven

Porcius and Socration
Piso's got two left hands
          (which what the right is doing never know)
and you're them
dandruff on the world's collar
hunger ache in its gut

are you the two
he put ahead of my good friends
Veranius and Fabullus?
must have been his old trouble
         (antsinthepants)
are you the ones who get the fancy dinners
         (what a wad he blew on those)
far far into the night?
and my friends V and F
are panhandling an invite
         to Greasy Joe's.

forty-eight

honeyed are your eyes, Juventius
and if someone would let me kiss them on
and on and on until I'd kissed
three hundred thousand times
I think I'd never feel I'd had enough
not if more dense than sun-baked fields of grain
should stand the crop of kissings we had made

forty-nine

Mister Orator one and Silver Tongued most only
of all the bastards Romulus begat
(count them all: the are, the were, Mark Tully,

and the willbe in the years that are to come)
a great big Vote of Thanks to You from Me
hereby recorded is and duly sent
you know me: poet of poets all the worst
just so much poet of poets all the worst
as you are lawyer of lawyers all the best

fifty

yesterday, Licinius, we had nothing to do
and so we amused ourselves at length
upon my writing-pad (we had agreed
to write on subjects not too serious)
we scribbled verses, both of us,
(picking whatever metre seemed to suit)
and handed them back and forth with a laugh and a drink.
and by the time I left for home, your charm
had set me blazing, Licinius, and your wit.
I tried to eat my dinner, but could not
I tried to sleep: peace would not roof my eyes
I was fairly wild. all over the bed
I tossed and turned—would daylight never come?—
I couldn't wait to continue our talk
and to just be with you again.
at last I grew tired of tossing and my limbs
lay scarcely alive upon my bed
it was then, dear friend, I wrote this poem for you
so you might see quite clearly how I suffered
now don't get tough! this is a prayer I send
I beg you, now, don't snort and push it aside

or Nemesis may turn her lash on you
she's a goddess with a temper
don't make her mad

fifty-one

he to me wholly godlike seems
he (please god forgive) seems higher than god
who sits across from you and over and over
          looks at you and hears you
sweetly laughing, miserably which all
my senses rips from me, for the minute Lesbia
I lay eyes on you nothing is left me
          of . . . . . .
but torpid my tongue, thinly down under my skin
flame trickles, with their own sound
roar my ears, twin night
          covers my eyes

fifty-one b

Catullus, it's bad for you to have nothing to do
when you've nothing to do you get all stirred up and excited
having nothing to do, in days gone by, has ruined
          kings and rich cities

fifty-two

Catullus, what you waiting for?
why not just drop dead?
the votes are counted
and look who's in
that pimple on the pratt of time
Nonius, and say have you heard
Vatinius says he really can't believe
(aw gee whiz guys) that come next january
he's gonna land smack in the consul's chair
Catullus, what you waiting for?
why not just drop dead?

fifty-three

laugh I thought I'd)
there was this guy in court, see
and we'd just heard a marvellous speech
against Vatinius: my friend Calvus
really'd thrown the book at him
well this guy LOVES it
gives him a great big hand
and says
boyoboy can dat lidl squoit
make wid duh lengwich

fifty-four

Otho's got the head of a cretin. . . . . .
*
. . . .and legs like a peasant, none too well washed
*
. . . .if I can't do everything, I'll hope to annoy
you and Fuficius, that old bird
who thinks he's a boy again. . .
*

no doubt you'll be angry again at these verses of mine
although you've no right to be, dear Generalissimo.

fifty-five

now please, if it isn't too much trouble
show me where you're hiding out
I looked for you in Little Park
I looked in all the bookstores
I looked in Father Jupiter's holy temple
  I went down Pompey's portico
  and grabbed onto every dame
  (at least the ones that looked fairly good-natured)
  . . . . and I kept saying to 'em
  "tell me if Jimmy's here, you tramps!"
  one of 'em yanks back her dress and says
  "Chemise? look, eet's 'ere, joost ondair
    my peenk teets

        bot eet nids bettair man as you
                to gat eet!"
aren't you being awfully snooty, friend?
come on, tell us where you're going to be
give, boy, give, let us in on it, tell the world
        those babes with the bosoms really got you?
        if you keep your tongue shut up in your mouth
        you'll lose half the fun of having a dame
        talk it up, boy! Venus likes palaver
well, o.k., lock up your lip if you want to
must be Real Love with you this time

fifty-six

funny?
O Cato, it was a LAUGH
I want you to hear it
I know it'll make you smile.
laugh, Cato, as you love Catullus, laugh.
it really is funny, it's just too rich:
just a minute ago I caught a little fellow
(belongs to my girl)
doing something in a corner
and—so help me Venus!—
without a knife to my hand
I cut him down to size
with a hard one.

fifty-seven

nice little set-up those bastards have got
darling Mamurra and Caesar dear
no wonder: the same brush tarred them both
one caught it at Rome and the other at Formiae
the spot sank right in and'll never wash out
(two little twins with the same disease
same sweet little school for their Ph.D.'s)
one's as bad as the other: just take your pick
they've started a partnership "Girlies, Inc."
nice little set-up those bastards have got

fifty-eight

Caelius
it's Lesbia, my Lesbia, that Lesbia
the Lesbia whom Catullus loved
more than self and all he calls his own
now at the corners
and down the back alleys
ashes she hauls ashes
for Father Remus' every bastard son

fifty-eight b

no, not if they made me into that sentry of Crete
no, not if I rode through the air on a Pegasus
no, not if I were Ladas or pinniped Perseus
no, not if I were Rhesus' swift snow-white team
          (add all the feathered feet and winged shoulders,
          look for the paths where the wild winds blow
          and catch them and turn them all over to me)
I'd still, friend, be tired in every bone
and sick and weary and worn to a frazzle
with looking and looking and looking for you

fifty-nine

Rufa's from Baloney-town
an' what she and little cousin Rufus
is doing together ain't pretty, boys
she's married, too, to a guy named Menenius
you seen her lotsa times out in the graveyards
snitching a dinner offa some poor guy's coffin—
fire gets goin', loafa bread rolls off,
she takes out after it
but some lousy undertaker's helper
catches her and beats the hell out of her

sixty

was it a she-lion on some Libyan mount
or Scylla with howling hounds where legs should be
that mothered on you a heart so hard and foul
that when a man begs for mercy in life's last hour
you treat him like dirt—O savage cruelty!

sixty-one

come from your hill, from Helicon,
come from your home, Urania's child
off to her husband steal the bride,
maid to her man, o wedding-god,
    O Hymen Hymenaeus 5

bind on your brow a flowered crown
of marjoram, the sweet-perfumed
put on the scarlet veil, be glad
glad as you come on snowy foot
    wearing the saffron sandal 10

come join us on our merry day
sing us the festal wedding-song
in little bell-tones high and clear
give us the beat to dance, lift up
    and swing the pine-torch blazing 15

here's Vinia, bride to Manlius,
(like Venus Idalian, on that day
she came before the Phrygian judge)
good virgin she, and good the signs
    that mark her day of marriage   20

call her a flower, call her bright
as any Asian myrtle-branch
that hamadryad elfin maids
plant in the garden where they play
    and nourish with the dew-drops   25

hither, then, Hymen, turn your steps
come, leave the land of Thespia,
the rock Aonian, and the cave
curtained by waters cool, where flow
    the streams of Aganippe.   30

summon the lady to house and home
for husband new her want awake
her heart with love bind all about
as ivy roving clings and folds
    the tree-trunk in its branches   35

and you too join us, pure and chaste
maids of honor (for you there comes
a day like this): take up the beat,
sing "Hymenaeus Hymen, O,
    O Hymen Hymenaeus"   40

gladden his heart when he shall hear
our prayer, for to the task he loves
we bid him turn and come this way,
the guide of holy wedded love,
     the yoke of pure affection.   45

what god is more besought in prayer
by lovers loving and beloved?
to whom do men more honor pay
in heaven? O Hymen, wedding-god
     O Hymen Hymenaeus   50

"bless me and mine!" in quavering tones
some ancient prays; "for thee we loose
the virgin's knot," our maidens cry;
fearful of you but eager too
     the bridegroom waits your coming   55

into a young man's bold hot hands
the fragile bloom of a budding maid
you surrender, though still she clings
to mother's arms, O wedding-god,
     O Hymen Hymenaeus.   60

without your blessing, love may take
no smallest profit that the world
would count as lawful, but it may
with your consent: who to this god
     would dare declare him equal?   65

without your blessing there's no house
can bring forth children, there's no sire
can hope for offspring, but they can
with your consent: who to this god
    would dare declare him equal? 70

the land that knew naught of your rites
could never bring forth guardians
to watch its boundaries, but it could
with your consent: who to this god
    would dare declare him equal? 75

draw back the bolts! fling wide the doors!
here comes the bride! the torches, see,
how shine and shimmer their fiery locks!
. . . .
    80

her maiden modesty slows her step
. . . .
to this she yet gives readier ear
. . . .
    she weeps that it's time to be going. 85

come, dry your tears! you run no risk,
Aurunculeia, that on the morn
some woman lovelier than you
may see the dawn send up its beams
    bright from the eastern Ocean 90

like you, in a rich lord's garden plot,
'mid all the colors massed and bright
stands out the bloom of the fleur-de-lis
but you're delaying: the hour is late
    come out, new bride, to your wedding!   95

come out, new bride, to your wedding now,
come, if you please, come out and hear
the song we sing: the torches, see,
how golden shimmering shine their locks
    come out, new bride, to your wedding   100

your husband, long as you both shall live,
will keep him only unto you
he'll do no wrong, no shameful thing
nor look to lie in other beds
    apart from your young body   105

no, rather, as the clinging vine
enfolds the tree that grows nearby
he will be close within your arms
enfolded—but the hour is late
    come out, new bride, to your wedding   110

o marriage-bed, that to all men
. . . .
. . . .
. . . .
    a bed's foot white and shining   115

what great delights are on their way
to your young master while the hours
of night speed by; what joys he'll know
at mid-day—but the hour is late
    come out, new bride, to your wedding   120

lift up your torches, boys, I see
the scarlet veil is on the way
come, take up the beat, together sing
"O Hymenaeus Hymen, O
    O Hymen Hymenaeus!"   125

this is the time (no holding back!)
to crack your bold Fescennine jokes
tell Pretty-boy he can't refuse
to give you nuts because he's heard
    dear Master doesn't love him   130

ya-a-a, Pretty-boy, come on and give
nuts to the boys; you've had your day,
you've had your fun: now comes the time
for you to serve the wedding-god
    Pretty-boy, scatter the walnuts   135

the other slaves were dirt to you,
Pretty-boy, only a day ago
now it's your face the barber comes
to shave—not quite so cocky now,
    Pretty-boy, scatter the walnuts   140

they tell us, husband, 'twill be hard
—you and your finery!—to keep clear
of your young smoothy—but keep clear!
O Hymenaeus Hymen O
    O Hymen Hymenaeus   145

we know that you have only known
what's lawful—but you're married now
and what is lawful's not the same
O Hymenaeus Hymen O
    O Hymen Hymenaeus   150

and you, too, bride, take care: don't say
"no" to what your husband will ask
or he'll go asking otherwhere
O Hymen Hymenaeus O
    O Hymen Hymenaeus   155

look, bride: the house! your husband's house!
how rich and powerful it is
say but the word, 'twill be your slave
(O Hymen Hymenaeus O
    O Hymen Hymenaeus)   160

until the day when old age comes
and palsy makes your hoary head
nod "yes" to all, to everything
O Hymen Hymenaeus O
    O Hymen Hymenaeus   165

lift up (good luck! don't stumble here!)
across the threshold your golden feet
pass through the shining doorway smooth
O Hymen Hymenaeus O
    O Hymen Hymenaeus   170

see there! within the house he lies,
your husband, on his Tyrian couch
waiting and watching all for you
O Hymen Hymenaeus O
    O Hymen Hymenaeus   175

for him no lower than for you
flickers within his heart of hearts
the flame, but deeper down it lies
O Hymen Hymenaeus O
    O Hymen Hymenaeus   180

let go the lovely rounded arm
of our sweet maid, young acolyte
up to the bride-bed let her come
O Hymen Hymenaeus O
    O Hymen Hymenaeus   185

and you, good matrons, whom your men
have loved so well for years and years,
come, lay our sweet maid in her bed
O Hymen Hymenaeus O
    O Hymen Hymenaeus   190

now, husband, come: it is your time
your wife lies in the bridal room
see how there shines upon her face
the white bloom of the maiden-flower
    the red glow of the poppy   195

but, husband, by the powers above,
you're no less handsome than your bride
our Lady Venus never thought
to scorn you—but the hour is late
    come on now, don't be lagging   200

ah, there you are! you haven't lagged
for long. may Holy Venus shed
a blessing on you, since your want
is honest want, and since your love
    is unconcealed and lawful.   205

who'd count the sands of Africa?
who'd number all the twinkling stars?
a man would sooner reckon up
their totals than he'd know the tale
    of times you'll sport together.   210

sport as you will, and may you soon
be blessed with children: it's not right
that any name as old as yours
should fail of children: let it be
    of offspring ever fertile   215

a tiny Torquatus I'd like to see
safe in his mother's circling arms
hold out his darling baby hands
and give to his father that first fleet smile
    with little lips half-parted   220

may he reflect his father's face:
a Manlius beyond all doubt
known on the spot by everyone;
and, for his mother, may he show
    her virtue by his features   225

and may he prove his mother's son
in goodness that will gain him praise
just as men called Telemachus
"the Good" and in his goodness saw
    Penelope, his mother   230

come, maids of honor, close the door
we've had our fun. Husband and wife,
we wish you every happiness
may health and youth and love and life
    bring you delights unending.   235

sixty-two

there's Vesper, boys: up! Vesper on Olympus
(how long we waited!) lifts his lamp at last
up, now, it's time! now leave the heavy board!
soon comes the bride, soon peals the wedding-song
O Hymen, wedding-god, come, Hymenaeus   5

look, maidens: see the boys! up with you, too
yes: over Oeta shines the Night-star's flame
that's right for sure: you see how quick they jumped?
nor aimless jumped: their song we'll have to beat
O Hymen, wedding-god, come, Hymenaeus   10

not easy, friends, the palm we hope to win.
see how the maidens con the lines they learned,
nor aimless con: they've got a Song to Sing.
no wonder! their whole mind is on their task.
we've listened with our ears but not our minds;   15
we're fairly beat, for victory loves care.
so now, at least, turn to with all your hearts
soon they will sing, soon we must make reply.
O Hymen, wedding-god, come, Hymenaeus

Hesper, what fire more cruel rides the sky?   20
you tear the daughter from her mother's arms
from mother's arms the clinging daughter tear
and give to a hot-blood youth the maid untouched
what act by foe in captured town more cruel?
O Hymen, wedding-god, come, Hymenaeus   25

Hesper, what fire more welcome lights the sky?
your flame will tie the knot of nuptial bonds,
by husbands, by fathers long since ratified,
yet never joined before you rise and glow.
what gift of god more blessed than this hour?   30
O Hymen, wedding-god, come, Hymenaeus

Hesper, dear friends, has stolen one of us
. . . .
. . . .
. . . .
. . . .
. . . .
(O Hymen, wedding-god, come, Hymenaeus)
. . . .
for when you rise, the city-watch awakes
by night the thief is safe, but you return
Hesper, with other name, and catch him yet   35
'gainst you, the maidens only feign complaint.
complaint? when in their hearts they long for you?
O Hymen, wedding-god, come, Hymenaeus

as grows a flower behind the garden-wall
unknown to oxen, by no plow torn up,   40
pet of the breezes, child of the sun and rain,
beloved of many a boy and many a girl,
yet let some dainty finger pluck its bloom,
beloved by never a boy and never a girl:
so is the maid, while chaste, while yet held dear.   45
but when her bloom is lost, her body stained,
nor sweet to boys is she, nor dear to girls
O Hymen, wedding-god, come, Hymenaeus

as grows a widowed vine on naked field,
ne'er rising up, ne'er showing the mellow grape,   50
but heavy her tender body bending down
laying her topmost twig close by her foot,
tended by never a farmer, never an ox,
but if she's joined in marriage to the elm,
tended by many a farmer, many an ox: 55
so is the maid, while chaste, while yet unloved.
when in due time she's formed a fitting match
her husband loves her more—her father, too.

you've a good husband, girl; now don't resist him
you mustn't resist: your father gave you to him,   60
father and mother, too; you must obey them.
your maidenhood you share with both your parents
a third's your father's, and a third your mother's
only a third is yours: don't fight the two:
your husband has their rights and has your dowry.   65
O Hymen, wedding-god, come, Hymenaeus.

sixty-three

over the deep rode Attis in a swift ship over the seas.
in Phrygia there stands a grove; to this he hastened and his
    foot tingled as he touched it.
he went in where it was dark with trees, a place clothed in
    forests, the place of the goddess.
and he felt a sting there and he raged and was mad and his
    mind wandered.

and he cast down the weights of his loins, with a sharp flint
    cast he them down.   5
now they were gone; he knew it, and that his body was with-
    out man.
even as fresh upon earth's soil lay the spot and stain of his
    blood
with hands that were white as the snow he quickly caught
    up the light tambour
(tambour, the trumpet of Cybele, whose tone bringeth man to
    thee, O Mother)
and he shook the bull's-back and beat it with fingers like
    those of a woman   10
and he raised his voice and sang to his followers, trembling
    sang he this song:

"come climb the heights, ye Gallae* to Cybele's woods with
    me
come with me fleet flock* of our Lady of Dindymus
into the places of other men* ye have come like exiles
in my train ye have followed where I led* with me have ye
    shared   15
the swift sea's trials* and the terrors of the main
your bodies ye have unmanned* for very loathing of love
with wildness of your hearts make ye glad* the heart of Our
    Lady
let there be no hanging back in your hearts* come with me
    where I lead
to the Phrygian home of Cybele* to the Phrygian groves of
    our goddess   20
where the voice of the cymbals is heard* and the tambours
    resound
where the flautist of Phrygia plays the note of doom* upon
    his rounding reed

where Maenads mightily toss their heads* (and they wear
    crowns of ivy)
where they lift their voices to scream* 'holy holy holy is thy
    Name'
where unceasingly the band of our goddess flies* and knows
    no rest   25
there must we haste* our hurrying dancing feet."

and when Attis had sung this song unto his followers (he was
    nor man nor woman now)
the choir suddenly with trepid tongue screamed
there was a light tapping and roll of the tambour, the hollow
    brass gave back a crash
and up the green hill of Ida dashed the dancers with fleeting
    foot.   30
for madness his breathing comes in gasps; hither and thither
    he runs; his heart heaves
the tambour is ever at his side; even thus did Attis lead
    through the darkness of the forest
(and he was like to the heifer that dodges the load, unbroken
    of the yoke)
with a rush the Gallae follow their leader, for he is swift of
    foot.
and thus into the house of Cybele they came, and they were
    wearied   35
for overmuch toil they took their sleep without bread
a numbness came over them and weariness in waves; they
    closed their eyes and slept.
and off from them departed in sweet rest the rabid raging
    of their hearts
but when the golden face of the Sun with the rays of his
    eyes
marked his circuit over white ether, hard earth, savage
    sea,   40

and put to flight the shades of night with the mighty pounding
    of his horses' hooves,
then did Attis awake for the Lord Sleep fled from him and
    hastened to depart
(upon her beating heart the Lady Pasithea received him)
and so was sweet rest gone and rabid rage no more
and now in his heart Attis told over the tale of his deeds   45
and with a mind clear of clouds saw what he had lost for
    ever and ever
his soul boiled up within him again, and he turned his path
    back to the waters of the sea
there it lay in all its hugeness; as he beheld it the tears
    started from his eyes
"land of my fathers!" he cried, and his heart was sore and
    his voice was the voice of one cast down
"land of my fathers, that gave me being, land of my fathers,
    O thou that gave me birth   50
I, 'tis I, have left (ah, woeful word!)—left thee as slaves
    their lords and masters flee
and towards Ida's groves have turned my foot
to be at home amid the snows and the wild beasts' icy dens
to go in mad search of their every hiding place
where, oh where, in what places, land of my fathers, do I
    deem thee to lie?   55
how longeth mine eye's very pupil to send its beam unto
    thee,
while savage madness is gone for one short hour from my
    heart
is it I who am gone from mine own, I who shall hie me to the
    wilds from the home that was mine?
homeland, hearth, friends, parents, shall I be gone from you
    all?
shall I be gone from the streets, the halls, the places where
    the young men meet?   60

O break, break, my heart, and raise again and again a sound
    of wailing.
for what shape of man is there that I have not put on?
a woman I, a young man I, a stripling I, a boy I
flower of the field-day I, and prize of wrestlers was I
mine were the doors where the young men thronged, mine
    the doorway their vigils kept warm   65
mine were the flowers and garlands that wreathed my house
when I had to go forth with the risen sun and leave my bed
am I now called waiting-maid of the gods and Cybele's slave?
a maenad I, half of myself I, a man unsexed, shall that be I?
I on green and icy Ida, in places clothed with snow, I a
    dweller?   70
I am to pass my life under the tall columns of Phrygia
with the doe, the forest-lover, with the boar, the wildwood-
    wanderer?
now, now am I grieved for that which I have done, now,
    now I repent, I repent."
from his red lips the sound swift passed away
and entered into the ears of the gods to bring them new
    report   75
and Cybele unfastened the yokes from her lions
and to the nigh ox-enemy she put the goad and spoke:
"begone," said she "begone! in all thy fury go, make madness
    drive him on,
make madness maul him till he turn back to my wilds
for he is too much the free man when he knows the wish to
    escape my power   80
come, beat thy back with thy tail; that lash is thine: lay
    on with it!
fill all the world with thy noise, and let it echo to thy roaring
shake thy ruddy mane—wild! wild!—and roll the rippling
    sinews of thy neck!"

thus spoke Cybele, and her wrath boded ill; and she slipped
   the latch from the yoke with her hand.
off went the beast, and his rage was spur and goad to his
   madness   85
he rushes he roars he crashes the thickets, his foot speeds
   ever on
and he came where the land lay wet and white with the
   foam of the sea
and beheld the unman Attis where he stood by the marbled
   main
he charged; Attis with the scream of a madman fled to the
   forest wild
and there for ever and ever all his life's course
   he was a slave.   90
      O Holy Mother* Lady of might
      O Holy Mother* Cybele
      O Holy Mother* Dindymus' Queen
      Grant that this house * where I dwell
      May never know the madness * thou canst send   95
Drive other men to frenzy* drive other men insane.

sixty-four

On Pelion's top one time were born the pines
(men say) that sparkling swam the Neptune-waves
to Phasis' floods and confines Aeetean,
when picked young men, oaks of the Argive youth,
the golden fleece of Colchis prayed to steal,   5
down the salt deeps dared race their nimble craft,

and swept the bright blue sea with piney palms.
for them the goddess of forts on city heights
herself made up the light wind flying car,
and joining a weft of deal to an inbent keel   10
first taught the unlettered Sea to be a road.

    Soon as her bow slashed through the windy plain,
and wrenched by oars the wave grew white with foam,
up faces rose from out the main's white swirl,
sea-daughters, Nereids, at the portent wond'ring.   15
that day, if e'er, men saw with mortal eye
the daughters of the deep, the naked nymphs,
breast-high uprising from the hoary swirl.
then Thetis' love (they say) made Peleus burn;
then Thetis scorned not the bridal-songs of man;   20
then Thetis, as Jove well knew, must Peleus wed.

    O blessed in time was the hour that saw your birth,
heroes; hail, sons of god, of mothers good
good progeny, hail once again! . . . . .
your names oft, often in my song I'll sing—
you most, richly with lucky torch endowed,   25
pillar of Thessaly, Peleus, to whom Jove himself,
himself the god-begetter gave his girl.
was't you that Thetis held, sea-child most lovely?
you that Tethys her grandchild gave to wed,
and Ocean, whose seas the whole wide world embrace?   30

    So soon in season due the longed-for days
have come, his home is meeting-place for all
Thessaly, holiday crowds his palace fill;
their hands bear gifts, their faces show their joy.
desert is Cieros, lorn are Tempe's vales   35
and Crannon's homes and ramparts of Larissa.
to Pharsalus, in Pharsalus' halls, they throng
none till the farms, soft grow the oxen's necks,

no curving rake-tooth cleans the low-hung vine
no bull with share down-pressed rips up the clod   40
no pruner's hook thins out the shade of tree
scaly the rust lies on forgotten plows.
but Master's home, wherever rich recede
his halls, is bright with gold and silver fulgent.
on couches ivory white, cups light the board,   45
the whole house joys, with royal treasure bright.
the bed where weds a bride divine is placed
in palace-midst; with Indian tusk it shines,
covered by rosy purple murex-dyed.
this cloth with ancient shapes of men adorned   50
of heroes bold tells tale with wond'rous art:
a maid looks forth from Dia's roaring shore,
and Theseus fleeing with fast fleet descries
wild is her heart—Ariadne 'tis—and mad
nor what she sees believes yet that she sees   55
for just now wakened from deceitful sleep
she knows herself left lorn on lonely sand.
Theseus forgot; he flees with splashing oars
his worthless words to windy tempest tossed.
he's far from shore; with sad eyes Minos' child   60
posed like a marble Maenad sees him go,
ah, sees, and ebbs and flows on floods of woe
not held by silken coif her yellow hair
not veiled her bosom by her dainty robe
not bound her milky breasts by cincture soft   65
all as they slipped from all her body lay
at her feet, the playthings of the wanton sea.
so stood she; for her coif and rippling robe
she cared not; all her heart on, Theseus, you,
and all her soul and all her mind hung dying.   70
poor maid! with endless pain Love bore her down

planting within her heart the thorns of care
that day and from then on when Theseus bold
standing out from the curved shores of Piraeus
to halls of a king unjust, to Gortyn, came.   75
    For—so they tell—once deadly plague compelled
payment of blood-price for Androgeos slain:
each year the best young men, the loveliest maidens
Athens must send, the Minotaur to banquet.
since woes like these her narrow walls tormented   80
Theseus his own life for his Athens dear
chose to renounce, that such to Crete no more
dead yet not dead from Cecrops' land be carried.
so sped on nimble ship and with light breeze
to mighty Minos' haughty halls he comes.   85
on him then glanced with light of love the maid
the princess (sweet the breath of chaste perfume
from bed where soft in mother's arm she lay,
pure as the myrtles by Eurotas born,
bright as the hues that dance in springtime breeze)   90
nor sooner from him bent her burning gaze
until each atom of her flesh caught fire
deep down, and her whole soul burst into flame.
ah me! with cruel heart you drive men mad,
lad holy, who lace their cup of woe with joy;   95
and you who Golgi rule and Cyprus leafy,
how have you tossed the girl with soul afire
on your waves, for fair-haired stranger often sighing?
how great the fears she bore with fainting heart
how paler oft she turned than gleam of gold   100
when eager against the savage Beast to fight
at death aimed Theseus or at glory's crown.
    Not unblest, yet in vain the gifts to god
she promised as with silent lip she prayed.

for as on Taurus' top shaking its arms   105
the oak, or cone-clad pine with sweating bark,
the wild wind, wracking with its blast their strength,
rips out (she from her deepest root uptorn
falls flat . . . . to break what blocks her way)
so Theseus tamed the Beast and laid him low: 110
his horns caught nothing but the empty air.
then back he turned unharmed and full of praise
guiding with slender thread his erring steps
lest as from twisting labyrinth he passed
the palace fool him with its puzzling maze.   115
    But why should I from earlier strain digress
to tell a longer tale, how daughter left
a father's face, a sister's arms, a mother's—
(poor soul: that ruined daughter was her joy)
how to all these dear Theseus she preferred;   120
or how raft-borne to Dia's foamy shore
she came, or how, her eyes enchained by sleep,
he left her, sailed, forgot her—he, her spouse.
often, men say, with heart aflame and mad
she shrieked and emptied all her breast of screams,   125
then woebegone climbed up the rugged rocks
to stretch her gaze across the sea's vast tide
then out to meet the rippling wavelets ran
the soft robe raising from her naked thigh
and spoke with broken heart her last lament   130
pouring from tear-wet lips her poor cold cries:
    "Was't thus you haled me—liar!—from my home
liar!—on desert strand to leave me, Theseus?
is't thus you've gone and paid no heed to god—
forgot?—I curse your cargo of broken oaths!   135
was there no thought could bend your cruel mind's
design, no mercy standing at your side

that your hard heart might will to pity me?
this is not what you promised then, and coaxed
and teased, this is not what you bade me hope—   140
no! happy wedlock, marriage, the maiden's prayer
all this to scattered scraps the cold winds blow.
now let no woman trust man's pledge of faith
let none expect they'll keep their plighted word
for when the itch of wanting rules their mind   145
they fear no oath, no promise they withhold;
but sate that lustful heart, slake once their thirst:
their word's forgot, their broken oath a shrug.
yet when you spun in the eye of death's whirlwind,
I saved you, and rather decreed a brother's doom   150
than fail you—you liar, you!—in your last hour.
for this the beasts shall tear my flesh, and birds
shall eat me and no dust entomb me dead.
what lioness whelped you in some lonely lair?
what sea begat and spat you from its surf?   155
what Syrtes, Scylla greedy, vast Charybdis,
you who pay such reward for sweet life saved?
if marriage with me made no appeal to you
for fear of your stern old father's cruel commands,
yet see: you could have brought me to your home   160
to be your slave, to serve with joyful toil,
your shining feet with waters clear to soothe
and purple covers on your couch to spread.
        "But why do I make vain moan to the heedless winds
(mad am I?) that with senses not endowed   165
can neither hear nor answer spoken words?
Theseus is now near half-way 'cross the waves
and on the empty strand no soul's to see.
Fate, you have passed all bounds! I die, yet you
are savage and to my moan will lend no ear.   170

O Jove almighty, would it had ne'er begun
would that Greek ships had ne'er touched Cnossan shores;
that, bringing dreadful award to savage bull
that lying sailor had not made fast on Crete
nor—villain!—beneath sweet beauty hiding cruel   175
design, had rested—foreigner!—in my home.
where shall I turn? from what hope take new heart?
to Ida's peaks return? ah, swirling wide
between us growls the sea's ill-tempered plain.
look to a father's aid? what! whom I left   180
to chase a youth red with my brother's blood?
with husband's loyal love myself console?
what! he's gone, in the swirl his tough blades bending.
besides, on the shore's no (lonely isle!) no roof,
no way out through the sea's encircling waves.   185
escape there is none, hope none: voiceless all
desert is all, all wears the face of doom.
yet shall my eyes not faint away in death
nor from my weary bones the senses part
before I pray the gods for vengeance due   190
and cry to heaven for help in my last hour.
wherefore, you Furies, who for men's deeds exact
full fine, about whose brows the snaky hair
lies coiled, hissing, sign of the wrath within,
hither, come hither, hear ye my complaints   195
that—woe is me!—from my heart's deepest coign
I wrench, helpless, aflame, with mad rage blind.
and since I speak in truth and from the heart,
do you not let my sorrow go for naught,
but may that mind which has marooned me here   200
bring death and tears to Theseus and his house."
    When from her woeful heart she'd poured these words
praying redress (uneasy) for cruelty cruel,

assent unchanging nodded heaven's king.
at this his nod the earth and rippling sea   205
shuddered and Ether shook his twinkling stars.
and Theseus? blinding murk o'ergrew his mind;
he forgot, and from his heart dropped the whole tale
of orders e'er now kept with steadfast mind:
no joyful sign he hoist for his sad sire   210
to show he'd safely raised Erechtheus' port.
for (so they say) when Aegeus to the winds
his son entrusted, sailing from Athens' walls,
he kissed the boy, and these last orders gave:

    "Son, only son, far sweeter than life to me,   215
son, whom I send perforce to a doubtful fate,
born, just born, in my life's fast failing years,
since fate of mine and your hot restless heart
tear you from me though loth—my tired eyes
are not yet sated with a son's dear form—   220
I'll not be glad nor with joy send you forth
you shall not fly the signs of happy fate
no, first I'll empty all my heart of moans
on my white head pour dirt, with dust befoul it
then dyed sails to your roving yard I'll bend,   225
for this my grief, this fire that burns my heart
calls for a canvas dark with Spanish rust.
but if Itonus' holy maid shall grant
(our people and Erechtheus' home she swore
to aid) that bull's blood spatter your right hand   230
then see you forget not, let my words live on
stored in your heart, let no time rub them out:
so soon your eyes shall raise our Attic hills
unclothe your ship, haul down her deathly garb,
up with white sails, lay to your halyards all,   235
that I may soonest see, be glad, know joy

once more, since you'll be home—blessed be the hour!"
    These words e'er now with constant mind he'd kept,
had Theseus; now like clouds by wind-blast blown
from lofty snowy mountain peak they're gone.   240
but Aegeus waiting watching from tower's top
(worried, his eyes dissolved in ceaseless tears)
soon as he caught sight of the bellying sail
down from the cliff headlong he threw himself
believing Theseus dead by cruel fate.   245
thus to a house that mourned a father's death
bold Theseus came: as Ariadne grieved
through his forgetfulness, so now grieved he.

    Thus then she watched his parting ship, and wept,
and bleeding at heart conned her scroll of care.   250
but from the other side young Bacchus flew
with satyrs and sileni, sons of Nysa,
Ariadne, seeking you: you fired his heart.

. . . .

glad then the maids, and whirled and madly danced
"evoe!" screaming, "evoe!" heads twitching, jerking.   255
part of them shook the thyrsus with veiled point
part hurled the ragged limbs from heifer torn
part were girding their bodies with writhing snakes
part eyed the box where symbols darkly lurked
symbols the world would know but never shall.   260
others pounded on drums with hands held high
or with round gongs a ringing dinging raised
many with horns hoarse-throated boomings blew
and screeched on Orient pipes a scrannel tune.

    Rich was the cloth with scenes like these bedight   265
which veiled embraced and clothed the bridal bed.

    When with these sights the youth of Thessaly
was filled, to the holy gods they turned to yield.

as with his breath some glassy lake at morn
the West Wind dimpling wakes the waves to motion   270
as Dawn comes out the door of the ambient Sun,
slowly at first by gentle breathing blown
they move along: light is their plash and gay
then with more wind they come e'er thicker and faster
and flash long crimson paths of floating light,   275
so then leaving the royal entrance-hall
each his own way with devious foot departed.

    After they'd gone, first down from Pelion's peak
to come was Chiron bearing woodland gifts.
for every field-born bloom, each mountain flower   280
that grows on Thessaly's peaks, or near her streams
springs at the West Wind's warm and fertile breath
these helter-skelter twined he brought in wreaths
so sweet so gay their smell the whole house laughed.

    Next here's Penios, leaving Tempe green   285
(Tempe girdled by forests overhanging)
to Naiads to be filled with Doric dance,
not empty-handed: roots and all he brought
tall beeches, and the lofty straight-stemmed bays
yes, and the nodding plane, and gentle sister   290
of Phaethon-all-in-flames, and airy cypress.
these all about the house he stacked and piled
so that the hall with soft leaves veiled was green.

    Behind him comes Prometheus keen of heart—
faint now the scars of the ancient penalty   295
which once, by flinty chain his members bound,
he paid in full hanging from cliff-top jagged.

    And then the Sire, his holy Queen, and children
arrived, leaving you, Phoebus, alone in heaven
you and your twin who dwells on Idrus' peaks;   300
for just like you your sister hated Peleus

and Thetis' wedding day refused to share.
    So soon on snowy chairs they bent their limbs
richly with varied feast was piled the board.
meanwhile shaking their bodies in feeble dance   305
their tale of truth the Fates began to sing.
their agued limbs were wrapped all 'round by robes
of white whose purple borders girt their heels
but red on snow-white hair their fillets lay
their hands at work unending plucked and pulled.   310
the left a distaff clad in soft wool held
the right then deftly pulled down strands and turned
and shaped them with the fingers, then the thumb
twisting them spun the spindle's balanced weight
while the ever-nipping tooth smoothed out the work   315
and to their dry old lips clung bits of wool
which till then on the smooth yarn had stood out.
before their feet white was the wool and soft
the fleeces safe in willow baskets laid.
these then worked at the wool while with shrill voice   320
they sang in sacred strain a song of fate
a song that with deceit no time shall charge:
    "O glory great, by valor greater still,
Emathia's guard, whose son shall crown your fame,
hear what on festive day the Sisters tell,   325
true prophecy; but showing the path of fate,
whirl spinning the yarns, you spindles, whirl.
    Now comes, to bring you what all men desire,
Vesper; now comes, with lucky star, your bride;
she'll melt your heart and flood your soul with love   330
then weary-faint with you will share her sleep
(smooth is her arm about your brawny neck)
whirl spinning the yarns, you spindles, whirl.
    No house has ever sheltered love like this

no love has lovers yoked with bond like this   335
that knits the hearts of Thetis and of Peleus.
whirl spinning the yarns, you spindles, whirl.
    Your child shall be Achilles void of fear
(the foe shall know his breast but ne'er his back).
oft shall he dash and run to win the race   340
and pass the step flame-fast of darting doe.
whirl spinning the yarns, you spindles, whirl.
    To him in war no man shall deem him like
when Phrygia with Teucrian blood shall drench her plains
and Troy—her walls so long besieged by war—   345
Pelops the Perjuror's third-in-line shall sack.
whirl spinning the yarns, you spindles, whirl.
    His excellent valor and his brilliant deeds
oft shall mothers proclaim o'er their dead sons;
they'll tangle and tear the hair on their white heads   350
and mar their flabby breasts with feeble fists.
whirl spinning the yarns, you spindles, whirl.
    For as the reaper lops the ranks of grain
and under sun-blaze yellow reaps the fields
he'll topple the sons of Troy with deadly blade.   355
whirl spinning the yarns, you spindles, whirl.
    Proof of his mighty deeds Scamander's wave
that with the Hellespont so quickly mingles;
his bed he'll block with slain bodies in piles
and deep though the waters mix them warm with gore.   360
whirl spinning the yarns, you spindles, whirl.
    Proof, too, shall be the booty paid to death
when round and high the heaped-up earthen tomb
shall take the snowy smitten maiden's limbs.
whirl spinning the yarns, you spindles, whirl.   365
    For when to tired Greeks fate gives the power
to loose the bonds of Neptune from old Troy

a lofty tomb shall run Polyxena's blood
(she before axe shall fall, host before steel,
to drop headless on crumpled knee, a corpse).   370
whirl spinning the yarns, you spindles, whirl.

    So come, as your hearts have hoped, come, yoke your
        loves.
take, groom, this goddess here in blessed bond.
go to your eager spouse at last, go, bride.
whirl spinning the yarns, you spindles, whirl.   375

    This maid at dawning light will show her nurse
that yesterday's fillet cannot span her neck
(whirl spinning the yarns, you spindles, whirl)
and, Mother, no fears, no tears: no quarrelsome girl
in lonely bed shall spoil your hope of babes.   380
whirl, spinning the yarns, you spindles, whirl."

    Such were the joys the Parcae then foretold
in song to Peleus, sung with heart inspired.
for then the gods were here; they visited
the homes of the Good and Great, and showed them-
        selves   385
to men who yet remembered how to pray.
oft in his gleaming shrine the Father came,
when festal days brought on his yearly rites,
to see on the earth an hundred oxen fall.
often swift Liber on Parnassus' peak   390
drove the Thyiads (they screamed, their tresses streamed)
when Delphians vying to haste from all their halls
led in the god with joy, while altars fumed.
often in war's death-dealing strife Mavors
or Lady of Triton swift, or Rhamnus' Maid   395
in presence cheered on the bands of men to arms.
but since the Earth was stained with crime and wrong,
and Justice from our greedy hearts took flight,

brother has drenched his hands in brother's blood
the moans of son for father dead have ceased   400
father has hoped to bury his first-born son—
free, then to seize a virgin daughter's bloom,
'neath innocent son has lain a mother foul,
foul, fearless of staining the gods her sires,
all good and ill, in evil mixture mad,   405
have turned from us the gods' just-dealing hearts.
wherefore they'll have no part in throngs like these,
nor let themselves be touched by shining light.

sixty-five

Hortalus!
It never ends. I'm weary, worn with grief,
and have no converse with the Learned Maids.
I cannot bring the Muses' children sweet
out of my soul's heart, such her tides of woe.
My brother! only now in Lethe's pool   5
his poor pale foot was met and wet and washed.
Troyland beneath the shores of Cape Rhoeteum
took him, crushed him and hid him from my sight

· · · · · · ·

never again, brother more loved than life,   10
shall I see you, but I shall love you always;
always the songs I sing shall mourn your death—
such strains as sang under the trees' thick shade
Daulias, weeping for Itylus dead and gone.
yet, Hortalus, though my grief is great, I send   15

to you this version of Callimachus.
You must not think that what you said to me
was thrown to the winds or slipped out of my heart
like a lover's apple, gift in secret sent,
which falls out from a virgin's bosom chaste   20
(poor thing! she hid it there and then forgot.)
Her mother comes, she leaps up, out it pops
and drops and slides down, down, and rolls away;
tears start; a guilty blush creeps up her face.

sixty-six

All the lights of the mighty world he knew;
where rise the stars he learned, and where they set;
how flames the sun, how runs, and disappears;
how pass the planets in their seasons fixed;
how Trivia slips 'neath Latmos' caves, beguiled   5
by sweet love's call to leave her lofty course—
Conon!—he saw me too at heaven's door,
from Berenice's head a golden lock
bright shining, that to all the host of gods
she promised, stretching forth her smooth white arms,   10
what time her king with wedding newly blessed
had gone Assyria's land to devastate.
(Sweet was the battle of the night; its scars
he bore, the trophies won from maid despoiled.)
Can it be? Do brides hate Venus? Or are parents   15
chagrined for naught by foolish formal tears
that fall like rain within the bedroom door?

So help me, it's a sham! so help me heaven!
This my Queen taught me, for oh! how she wept
when her new husband went forth to grim war—   20
or did you grieve not for a bed left lorn,
but shed those tears to see a brother go?
How deep the care that gnawed your inmost heart,
how in that hour did worry fill your breast,
till you swooned dead away! and yet for sure   25
I knew you fearless from your childhood days.
Did you forget how bold you wrought to gain
a royal consort: was ever other so brave?
But then how sadly you bade your prince farewell;
how often—Jove!—your hand brushed at your eyes!   30
What god had power to change you? or do lovers
hate it when that dear body's far away?
Then in your loved one's name to all the gods
you promised me (not without blood of bulls)
if only he should return. In no great time   35
he'd added captive Asia to Egypt's bounds.
For these blessings the heavenly throng I joined,
just now received to pay an antique vow.
Unwilling, o Queen, I parted from thy head,
unwilling, I swear it by thee and by thy life!   40
Cursed be he who'd make such vow in vain,
yet who would claim himself as strong as steel?
Why, even that mount was overturned, the highest
o'er which the shining child of Thia rides,
when the Medes made a new sea, and their young men,   45
barbarians all, through Athos sailed their ships.
What strength has hair, when such things yield to steel?
Jupiter, damn thou the whole Chalybian race,
and him who first sought mines beneath the earth
and learned to forge the hardness of cold steel!   50

Not long cut off was I; my sisters yet
were mourning my demise, when Memnon's twin
beating the breezes with his fluttering wings
came to me. . . . Arsinoë's winged steed,
took me and carried me through the darkling air   55
to lay me down on Venus' holy lap.
Him for this task our Lady of Zephyris chose,
sojourner Greek upon Canopic shores,
. . . . . that not alone at heaven's door
the golden crown from Ariadne's brow   60
should hang, but that I too might shine out there
a votive offering spoiled from your fair head.
Moist with your tears I came where dwell the gods;
amongst old stars Our Lady placed me new,
near Virgo and near savage Leo's lights,   65
next to Callisto, daughter of Lycaon;
westward I move; slow lags the Herd behind
to sink at long last in the Ocean deep.
Yet though by night I feel the tread of gods,
and Dawn to hoary Tethys brings me back   70
(forgive me, Maid of Rhamnus, for these words:
there is no fear can make me hide the truth;
not though my fellow-stars hate and revile me,
will my true heart keep back what's treasured there)
my pain exceeds my joy, for I am gone   75
yes, gone forever from my Lady's head.
With her, while she was yet a child. . . . . .
. . . . . . with her the perfumes that I drank!
Now you for whom the nuptial day has come,
yield not your bodies to your loving husbands   80
nor cast your dress aside nor bare your breasts
before the oil-flask pays me the drops I love
—the flask of only you whose beds are chaste.

But she who's given to foul adultery,
vain be her gifts! The light dust drink them all!   85
I seek no offerings from unworthy hands.
No, no, dear brides! Let everlasting peace,
let everlasting love dwell in your homes!
But, you, my Queen, when you look toward the stars,
and on her feast days pray to Lady Venus,   90
let me not pass ungifted of perfume—
for I am yours—nay, flood me with sweet gifts!

      Stars, let me go! A Queen's lock I would be:
so might Orion beside Aquarius shine!

sixty-seven

"Well, well! it's the Husband's Friend, the Father's Friend!
Hello there! May God shed his grace upon you,
Door; they tell me that you served Balbus well
in time gone by when the old man owned the place,
but didn't serve his son so well, they say,   5
when the old man died and you took on a wife.
Come on, tell me: how come they say you changed,
and welshed on the trust your master placed in you?"

"As I hope Caecilius likes me (I'm his, now),
it's not my fault, no matter what they say.   10
I did no wrong; no one can say I did;
but people always say, 'the door's to blame!'
Yes, if they find some dirty trick's been played,
they all come shout at me, 'Door, that's your fault!'"

"No, that won't do; you can't just say it's so;   15
you've got to show us proofs; we've got to see."

"How can I; and who cares? who wants to know?"

"I do; come on, don't hesitate, speak up."

"Well, first, they say we got a virgin bride:
no sir; her husband didn't get her first—   20
that languid sickly good-for-nothing lump,
he'd never make the grade—not half-way up.
No, it was Papa fouled up Sonny's bed,
I hear, and filled this wretched house with shame.
Why? He was a bad old sinner—love is blind—   25
or maybe his son just couldn't measure up,
and someone had to be found with something more,
who'd have the strength to loose the virgin's knot."

"God, what a father: that's real loyalty
to push himself in where his son belonged!"   30

"But that's not all that Brixia says she's learned
(Brixia, planted under Tower Hill,
yellow where flow the Mella's gentle streams
Brixia, mother beloved of my Verona)—
no there's Postumius and Cornelius, too,   35
with whom our bride played fast and loose in love.
Someone might say, 'Door, where'd you learn all this?
You couldn't leave your Master's vestibule
to hear the people talk: you're fastened here;
you close and open up the house, that's all.'   40
I've heard her often slipping whispered tales
alone to her maids about these escapades,

and mentioning names—the ones I said: she thought,
you see, I couldn't talk or hear a thing.
She mentioned another man, too; I won't tell   45
his name, for fear he'd scowl: those red eyebrows!
(He's tall; he got sued once for all he had
for fathering some non-existent brat.)"

sixty-eight

What? to ME?
    By fortune's fall downcast in bitterness
    you wrote it all with tears your letter sent?
    "Shipwrecked, cast out by foaming ocean-waves"
    you I should "lift and from death's door bring back?"
    whom "holy Venus no soft rest in sleep   5
    desert on bed of bachelor allows?"
    and "of old sweetly written song the muse
    delights not when your heart with worry wakes—"
    I thank you, since 'tis me you call a friend,
    and "gifts o' the Muses" of me ask, "and Love."   10
But Manlius:
    you my tale too should know of grievances.
    I do not scorn (think not!) what friends should do.
    Hear how I drown in fortune's floods myself,
    and cease from grief the gifts of joy to ask.

    In days when first my gown was changed to white, 15
    happy when life blooming her Spring led on,

freely I roamed (Love is not deaf to me
who sweet into heartache mingles bitterness.)
But all this bent, grief at my brother's death
stole. O woe! O brother gone from me!   20
You when you died smashed all my worth, brother;
along with you wholly's entombed our House;
each one with you, with you died every joy,
which you in life sweet nourished with your love.
At your Passing from my whole soul I drove   25
these fancies, all these darlings of the heart.

So when you write, "Verona? shame, Catullus!
You there? when here each johnny better-heeled
chilly on empty warms, his limbs, your bed?"
This, Manlius, is no shame—it's just—toobad.   30

Your pardon then if what my grief destroyed,
these gifts, I do not send you, for I can't.
My books, you know—I haven't many here,
and that's because I live at Rome. That's house,
that's home to me; that's where I pluck my hours;   35
here from those shelves one armload followed me.

This being so, don't think that through ill-will
I act thus, or through breeding not the best,
that to your asking came no flood of Both.
Unasked I'd brought them had I but the power.   40

I can't but tell, Muses, how Allius
helped me or with what deep devotion helped,
lest fleeing ages down forgetting years
this that was his in blind night hide, his love.

But I'll tell you, you then shall tell to many   45
thousands and make this screed speak when in eld
. . . .
that he be famed yet more in death and more,
nor sheerly woven airy spider's web
on desert Allius' name its task perform.   50
For mine what gift from two-fold Love, what care
you know, and in what wise She ruined me,
when I was fever-hot as Aetna's peak
and Malic springs of Oeta's Thermopylae.
Sadly with tears my eyes forever wasted,   55
nor ceased a mournful rain to wet my cheeks,
as high in the air sparkling on ridge of mount
a rill all mossy leaps forth from a stone
(when down, down, headlong from the vale it rolls,
straight through the crowd it cuts the peopled road,   60
sweetly the traveller's weary sweat to ease
when heavy the scorching heat makes pant the fields)—
here, as to sailors tossed in tempest black
a gentler breath of wind and favoring comes
("Help, Castor! Pollux, help!" their prayer they made) 65
such was to me my Allius, such his aid.
He oped the gate upon a wide-wayed field;
he gave a house to me, he gave to Her,
where we might share the doing of our Love.
Here 'twas that softly white my goddess' foot   70
came; where the sill was worn her shining sole
she planted; creaked her sandal as she stood.
A husband's love as once enflaming brought
to Protesilaus Laodamia home;
a bridal vain, for yet no holy blood   75
of sacrifice had soothed the lords of heaven
(nought may I so much want, Rhamnusian Maid,

that's rashly done without the lords' consent).
How thirsts the shrine to drink of pious blood
Laodamia learned from husband lost,   80
a bridegroom's love compelled to send away
before the coming of one year and two
in night's long hours eager her love might sate,
that she could live though marriage broken lay.
And this (so wot the Fates) was not far off   85
if he a soldier went to Ilian walls.
For then, with Helen raped, the Argive chiefs
first heard Troy call them to her, those great men—
Troy (shame!) where Asia and Europe shared a tomb,
Troy, all men's and all valor's bitter ash.   90
Which to my brother too a wretched death
brought—ah, woe, ah brother gone from me,
ah, sad, a brother's well-loved light all gone;
along with you wholly's entombed our House;
each one with you, with you died every joy,   95
which you in life sweet nourished with your love.
You're so far off; not mid familiar tombs,
nor near your own your ashes laid to rest,
but in Troy, filthy, luckless Troy you lie,
held at end-of-the-world in alien soil.   100
There then hasting (men say) the gathered youth
of Greece their homes deserted and their hearths,
that Paris make not free of stolen joys,
taking his hours of ease in chambered peace.
Then, lovely Laodamia, came that blow   105
that stole from you than life more sweet and soul,
your spouse: so great the sucking swirl of love,
the tide that bore you steep into the gulf.
So deep (Greeks tell) near Pheneus and Cyllene
the drain that milks the fat soil of a swamp,   110

which once He sliced a mountain's heart to dig,
whom fame false-fathers on Amphitryon,
what time Stymphalian monsters with sure shaft
he pierced at bidding of a worser lord,
that o'er heaven's gate more feet divine might pass   115
and Hebe keep not long her maidenhood.
But than that gulf your deep love was more deep,
which taught you, then untamed, to bear the yoke.
For not so dear to weary aged sire
that late-born babe at his one daughter's breast,   120
who, marked at last for Old Grandfather's wealth,
his name has placed on Will and Testament
(he mocks the selfish kinsman, joyless now,
and drives the vulture from that hoary head).
Nor so much in her snowy mate e'er joyed   125
the dove who far more wantonly is said
kisses with ever nipping beak to pluck
than that most-wanting woman of them all.
But these great passions were as nought to yours,
when once to your fair husband you were joined.   130
To you she needed nothing yield—or near—
My Light, when to my waiting arms she came
(about her hither-thither Cupid coursed
all white and shining in his yellow gown).
And though she's not content with me alone,   135
the lapses of my modest miss I'll bear
(I would not be a nuisance and a fool).
Oft even Juno, greatest of heaven's host,
by husband wronged swallows her burning ire,
knowing the All-Wanter's many thefts—that Jove!   140
(still 'tis not right men to gods to compare
. . . .
. . . .
thankless the load from agued sire lift off).

Yet not to me by father giv'n away
to sweet Assyrian-perfumed home she came:
no: stolen she gave (ah, wonder!) gifts by night   145
right from husband, slipped from his very arms.
So it's all right, to me if given sole
that circled date she names true holiday.

I've done the best I could: this gift of verse
for all your, Allius, kindnesses I pay,   150
that on your name scabby may form no rust
as this and that and other years go by.
To this add Heav'n all blessings Themis erst
in antique time bestowed upon the good:
blest be you all together: you, Your Life,   155
your house, in which my Lady and I knew love,
and he who first to us. . . . .
by whom were first engendered all our joys,
and far before all dearer to me than self,
My Light: as she lives, life is sweet to me.   160

sixty-nine

Rufus!
you got no business bein' surprised
if there's no dame that wants to lay
her nice white smooth leg under yours
not even if you break her down
by buyin' 'er some fancy clothes
or maybe a pretty-pretty, say,
that's got a big fat sparkler on it.

you know what 'tis that's hurtin' you?
well, there's a story goin' 'round
—jus' tellin' you what people say—
you got a goat, a stinkin' goat
lives in your armpits—yeah, that's what
the dames is scared of—and why not?
a goat's a dirty beast, no girl
is gonna wanta sleep with that

so either kill the thing that kills their noses
or quit your wonderin' why they run away

seventy

nobody
my Lady says there's nobody
she'd rather marry than me
not if Jove himself should come asking her
so she says
but what a woman says to a lover
that wants her
she should write on wind and running water

seventy-one

sometimes things is so right
you take a guy gotta stinkin' goat
      under his arm
or one got his comuppance (all cripple up)
      with the gout:
the guy that beat you outa yer gal
      and is doin yer Exercizes fer ya
boy it's wonderful—he stepped
      inta yer shoes caught
      both them troubles.
everytime they do it he makes
      both her and him
      pay for what he done to ya:
he kills her with the Stink
and himself with gout.

seventy-two

you used to say
(that was, oh, long ago)
that Catullus was the only man
you wanted to know,
Lesbia, and that before me
you would not wish Jove's own embrace.
my feelings for you then were not just those

that anybody has for a girl he'd make love to
but like those of a father for his sons
or for the fine young men that married his daughters
now I know what you are
yet though my desire for you flames
more wildly than ever, still
you seem to me more and more
like some poor worthless, thoughtless thing.
how can that be, you say?
because when a man's in love
and you hurt him the way you hurt me
it stokes his lust
but chills his heart

seventy-three

Stop!
don't think it about anybody
nobody earns the right to be loved
nobody knows what's meant by loyalty
thanks?
you don't get it anywhere
doing kindnesses?
what for? nobody cares
they think it's just a bore
a bore and a nuisance, that's what
just look at me
nobody's going after me more hot and heavy
than the one who not more than last week
called me his One and Only Friend

seventy-four

Gellius had always heard
how his uncle blew his top
if anybody talked about
the girls or made love to 'em

"can't have that happening to me"
said Gellius, and so he took
his uncle's wife and worked her over
and did that shut the old boy's mouth!

Gellius' got his uncle now
right where he wanted him, for if
he laid his uncle out himself
dear uncle couldn't say a word

seventy-five

look down down
if you want to find my heart, Lesbia.
you brought it down
it killed itself trying to do
what hearts are supposed to do
now it couldn't love you
if you were virtue in person
nor cease to want you
if you did everything

seventy-six

it's true isn't it
when people think back on the good things they've done
there's pleasure in it
        (you did what was right
        you kept your word
        you never took god's name in vain
        in order to cheat your fellow man)
then you've got lots to look forward to,
Catullus, in life's long years ahead
it was a love that knew no gratitude
but out of it great joy will come to you
for whatever, kindly, men to any man can say
or do, you said, you did
and all to a thankless heart entrusted died
why why then longer cut and lash yourself
in heart be hard, from where you are come back
the gods say no? well stop it anyway
its hard long suddenly love to lay aside
its hard but do it any way you will
this only health, this win, win on, win through
do this if this you can't, if this you can

        god if you know mercy
        if to any ever
        at the final door of death
        you've given the strength that saved
        me wretched look upon
        and if my life was good
        let this sickness pass
        this death let pass from me

down, under, down, the creeping numbness dulls
outdriven out of all my soul delight
I ask no longer that she love me too
or (anyway she can't) that she be pure
for my own health I hope and to lay down
the burden of this filthy foul disease

      god dear god grant me this
      for I was loyal ever

seventy-seven

Rufus, I thought you were my friend
but it was all no good and for nothing
for nothing? that's hardly right
it came very high and cost me plenty
so that's the way you sneaked up on me
stuck a red hot poker in my guts
and robbed me of everything that matters
you robbed me, all right
you poison of my life
you Thing
that made our friendship
sicken and die

seventy-eight

Gallus, Gallus, got two brothers
one's got a very handsome wife
the other's got a handsome son

that Gallus, he's a pretty one:
saw his chance to make a match
pretty boy and pretty girl:
tucked them in one pretty bed

Gallus, Gallus, he's a fool
did he forget he's got a wife?
isn't uncle showing uncle
how to play little bedroom games?

seventy-eight b

. . . .
this is what hurts me now
here's an innocent girl
getting her innocent kisses
all slobbered over with your filthy spit

by god, you won't get away with it
every age to come will hear of you
and Time will still be telling your tale
when she's a grey-haired Lady

seventy-nine

Lesbius is Mr. Fine
he's Fine all right; why, after all
Lesbia'd rather have him
than you, Catullus, and all your family
Fine he is, but he can put you, Catullus,
and all your family on the block
if he can find three men he knows
who'd shake him by the hand

eighty

Gelly-gilly
Daffy-dilly,
prithee, why so pale?
in the morning
in the evening
it's the same old tale.

something's doing
something's brewing:
what is this I hear?
weren't our kisses
meant for misses?
yours are not, I fear.

how'd I know it?
do you show it?
here's the pitch, my friend:
Victor's dying
Victor's crying,
"what a painful end!"

eighty-one

Juventius!
with all the people in the world
and all the handsome guys
you might have picked,
why pick that hick
from a town they haven't got around
to buryin' yet? an' he looks like
six feet of earth would do him good
he won your heart? you had the gall
to set him up ahead of me?
what a crime
this time

eighty-two

Quintius, if you want Catullus
to owe his very sight to you
(or anything else that's dearer still
than very sight)
don't take from him this thing which is
far dearer than very sight to him
(or anything else that's dearer still
than very sight)

eighty-three

when Lesbia's husband's by
oh my!
the dreadful things she says of me!
and he, the silly fool,
is happy as a lark
you stupid ass, you've got no sense
if she'd forgotten me
and didn't mention me
she'd be o.k.
but now she snarls and gabbles away
that means she's got me on her mind
not only that
but much more to the point
she's quite burned up at me

where there's talk
there's desire

eighty-four

to Arrius, "advantage" was "hadvantage"
always and every time, and "ambush," "hambush"
he thought his accent was its wondrous best
when he had given out a sounding "Hambush"
no doubt it's an ancestral trait—his mother,
his blue-blood uncle, grandpa, grandma, too
("on Mother's side, of course") all talked like that.

they sent him off to Syria; our ears
all took a rest; we heard those same words spoken
softly and smoothly in the Latin way
we thought we'd never hear such talk again
when suddenly here comes the awful news:
the Ionian Sea, once Arrius had got there
"Ionian" was no longer, but "Hionian."

eighty-five

I hate and I love
well, why do I, you probably ask
I don't know, but I know it's happening
and it hurts

eighty-six

who? Quintia?
she's the one so many people say
is beautiful?
nice complexion, nice proportion, nice build:
yes, I agree to all of that
but "beautiful?"
no, this I can't admit, no, not at all
why not?
she's got no personality
look at her: fine figure of a girl
but not a sparkle in her anywhere.
who *is* beautiful, then?
why, Lesbia, of course
in person, of all women loveliest
in heart, the charm she steals from all the rest

eighty-seven

no woman can ever say
that she was loved so much
(that is if she tells the truth)
as you were loved by me
            my darling
no loyalty was ever
in any bond so great
as in my love for you
on my side was discovered

eighty-eight

Gellius, dear Gellius
pray tell me what you'd call
a man who for his mother
and his sister Gave his All,
who wouldn't let his uncle
be a husband to his aunt—
can you such antics comprehend
or name—I'll bet you can't.

I'll tell you: all of Ocean's streams
from here to far Cathay
could never make him clean again
or wash his sins away
there is no greater depth of sin
to which a man could fall
not if he'd kiss his own sweet self
and Give himself his All.

eighty-nine

"poor Gellius is SO thin!"
why wouldn't he be?
what with a mother so Good to him
and a husky, handsome sister, too,
and my! how kind dear Uncle has been!

and the place is full of his cousins and aunts
how—but How?—could he help being thin?
assume just this: he touches nothing
but what he's not allowed to touch
you'll find a thousand reasons why
poor Gellius is so thin.

ninety

let's just suppose a nice incestuous pact
twixt Gellius and his mother: they'd produce—
a wizard, naturally, and he could learn
to be a Wise Man of the Orient
(well, that's what should be born to son and mother
if Persia's filthy cult is really true)
then how the gods will love him when he chants
and prays and melts the gut-fat in the fire!

ninety-one

Gellius I never thought
that you'd stay loyal to me
(when this love of mine
went bad and was lost)
because we'd been fairly intimate

or because I considered that you
were pretty steady, or that you
didn't even like to think of dirty deals

no, it was because I knew
that the girl I was eating my heart out for
wasn't mother or sister to you.
it's true that you and I
had been together quite a lot
but I didn't think that that would be
enough excuse for you

but you did: you get such supreme joy
out of doing what's wrong, whatever it is,
especially when it's a bit
on the snide side

ninety-two

Lesbia's always
scolding at me
she just simply can't
keep quiet about me
know what I think?
I think she loves me
and what's my proof?
I've got the same tally
I've never a word
of kindness for her

but know what I think?
I think I love her

ninety-three

JULIUS CAESAR
YOURE A SNOT
I DONT GIVE A DAMN
IF YOU LIKE ME OR NOT
MAYBE YOURE GOOD LUCK
MAYBE YOURE BAD
I DONT CARE
            (now go on and be mad)

ninety-four

Dickie-boy Trill loves somebody's wife
o somebody's wife loves Dick
            which is just so
            (as who doesn't know)
as to say that a sticker will prick

ninety-five

the "Zmyrna's" out!
Cinna has finished it
nine harvests
nine winters
since the day he began it
while Hortensius turns out
five hundred thousand verses
in a single . . . .
. . . .
the "Zmyrna" will travel
to where Satrachus rolls
his bottomless waters

the "Zmyrna" will be read
when Time is old and grey

but Volusius' "Annals" will die
at Padua where they were born
and make good wrapping
for fish-in-a-poke

the monument of my friend
is small but dear to me
no matter how much the mob
may shout for joy
at that blabber-mouth
Antimachus

ninety-six

if anything when words are heard no more
can gratefully by the grave yet be received
from this our—
(Calvus, shall I call it Grief,
this Missing-something
of a bygone day
painting afresh the years of youth and love
this Tear
we shed for friendships long since lost)—
surely her death untimely brings less pain
to your Quintilia than it wakes her joy
in knowledge of the love you bear for her.

ninety-seven

you take that guy Aemilius:
he's one of whom you'd say
you couldn't tell which end was up—
a stinker either way

in fact, I am inclined to think
I like him upside down
just slightly more than right side up—
for I can't see his frown,

his ugly mug with foot-long fangs
and gums like rotten leather;
and when he smiles, you'd think it was
a cess-pool in hot weather.

but he's the guy that loves the gals
a Devastating Male—
my God, when will they catch the man
and lock him up in jail?

why, any girl that would so much
as look at him—I'd say
she'd lick the hangman's running sores
and kiss the pus away.

ninety-eight

you are the man (if anybody is)
you stinker, Vettius, that we could tag
with the label we stick on fools that talk too much:
"The Tongue"—why, if you had to, you could use it
to lick the roughest toughest stuff in shape.
you want to kill us all in one fell swoop?
just open your mouth: in one fell swoop you've done it.

ninety-nine

I stole from you, my coy Juventius honey,
a kisslet sweeter than ambrosia sweet
but I was punished: longer than an hour
fixed on a cross was I—well I remember!
but all my pleas for pardon, all my tears
took not a tittle from your cruel wrath.
scarce had I kissed you when you splashed your lips
with water and scrubbed and rubbed them with your fists
that no contagion from my mouth remain
like the foul spittle of some filthy tramp.
then you consigned me to a cursed love
over and over, and tortured me so sore
that from ambrosia changed that kiss became
more bitter than the bitterest gall to me.
since this is the fine you levy on poor love
never again your kisses will I steal

one hundred

Caelius   Quintius
           loves
Aufilenus   Aufilena
      (they're the lilies of Verona)
the one   the other
         has got
the brother   the sister
      (a real sweet brother-and-sister act)
who should I wish more luck to: Caelius, you
the things you did proved you my one true friend
when madly a searing flame burned in my heart.
good luck Caelius, and win the game of love

one hundred one

many the peoples and many the seas
      I travelled through
and here I come poor prayers for the dead,
      brother, to say
to give you the last gifts of death
your speechless (and to what end) ashes to address
you are not here
fate took the You from me
o poor
it wasn't right

brother, you're gone from me
but now there's this to do
      (in days long gone our fathers laid it down
      and taught us the sad office of the dead)
here, take these gifts, wet wet with brother's tears
and for all time to come
brother
goodbye

one hundred two

some people—a rare confraternity—
can hold their tongues when trusted by a friend
with some deep secret; we know who they are.
count me initiate of their loyal band,
Nepos, and think me silent as the tomb.

one hundred three

dear Silo:
      may I have my money back?
then you may be bad-tempered as you please.
or if you like my cash, please, sir, don't be
a double-dealer and bad-tempered too

one hundred four

you think that I could speak ill of my Life
than both my eyes who's dearer far to me?
I couldn't, could I, and still love her so?
but you—perversion is your stock-in-trade.

one hundred five

Dickie-boy Trill
climbed helicon hill
to fetch a pail a poesy
the muses saw
and (being quick on the draw)
they knocked him arsover noesy

one hundred six

a man who sees a pretty boy
walking with a salesman,
what should he think but that the boy
was looking for a buyer?

one hundred seven

if anyone has a Want and a Wish
and then it comes
when he never thought it would
he gives it a real warm welcome
in his heart
that's why this is welcome to me
and richer than gold
that you've come back, my Lesbia
to my Want
come back to my Want and to my Unhoping
all on your own come back to me
brighter than bright the mark of this day
than me what man's more happy
or what man could name
a Wish more wished for
than a life like mine?

one hundred eight

Cominius, if the people took a vote
and sent your hoary halo of white hair
with every spot of moral muck still on it
down to the grave, I'll tell you what I think:
first off, the tongue that hated all good men
would be cut out to stuff a buzzard's craw

they'd dig out your eyes and throw them to the crows,
your guts to the dogs and to the wolves the rest.

one hundred nine

"happy" my darling, you say, "shall be this love,
    now and forever and ever between us two"
god grant her power to make this promise true
    to say it in honesty and from the heart
that we may honor so long as we both shall live
    this bond eternal, holy, cherished, dear

one hundred ten

Aufilena, you take these honest dames—
people always got a good word for them:
they make you a price, they stick to it.
but you—you made me a promise
and told me a lie, so you're
no friend of mine, and as
for your taking my money and then
not giving—that's a plain crime.

now Aufilena, either be a lady
and set your price, or be
a virgin pure, who'd make
no commitments at all.
but this business of taking and cheating
is worse than what some
girl in the business would do
that offers herself for sale
from top to toe.

one hundred eleven

Aufilena, to be content
to live with just one man
for brides is praise
of praises glorious.
but it's fairer for any woman
to lie with any man
than for a wife and mother
to bear cousins by her uncle

one hundred twelve

Naso, you're a busybody
and when you go to town
everybody's much too busy
to help escort you down

Naso, you're a busybody
why are your friends so few?
you've got, besides a tongue so busy,
a busy body, too.

one hundred thirteen

when Pompey first sat in the consul's chair
      (Cinna, oh, Cinna!)
two chappies there were found Maecilia fair
      (Cinna, oh, Cinna!)
now Pompey's been chosen a consul once more
      (Cinna, oh, Cinna!)
and the two are still there just the same as before
      (Cinna, oh, Cinna!)
but for each a full thousand have entered the field
      (Cinna, oh, Cinna!)
from two little seeds what a glorious yield!
      (Cinna, oh, Cinna!)

one hundred fourteen

Dickie-boy Trill has got a farm
at Fermo and rich is he
for on that farm he has a
            birds
Dickie-boy Trill has got
            fishes
a farm at Fermo
            cows
and rich is he
            oxen
Dickie-boy Trill
            boars
has got a
            (with a moo-moo here and a tweet-tweet there)
but I regret to state
he's no richer than before
the costs (which he forgot to remember)
are always somehow more
            (with an oink-oink here)
than what comes in
            (here a moo there a tweet)
so it's all right with me
for him to be so rich
so long as he hasn't a nickel
            (with an oink-moo here)
to rub against a dime
            (and a tweet-oink there)
and of his farm I'll sing
                        I hope it brex
                        his silly nex

one hundred fifteen

Dickie-boy Trill's got thirty acres of grass
and forty of grain, the rest is watery deep
why shouldn't he boast that he's richer than Croesus? he
    could:
in one fine lot he's got such a pile of wealth
pastures and grain-fields, forests and meadows and swamps
from here to the North and from there to Ocean's streams
it's all pretty big, but he beyond all is the biggest—
man? who said "man"? just great big old dangerous Dick.

one hundred sixteen

it was for you I worked and searched and hunted
that I might send you songs by Battus' son
to make you hate me less, make you refrain
from hurling death-darts ever at my head.
but no, that time was wasted, I can see,
Gellius, and my prayers to no avail.
well, hurl away! my guard is up against you
but I'll wound you and bring you to your knees.

notes

The numbering of the Notes refers to the poem numbers.

1. *Patron Maid:* Scholars disagree as to whether
   Catullus meant by this phrase one of the
   Muses (Euterpe, Erato, or perhaps Poly-
   hymnia) or Pallas Athena-Minerva, patroness
   of poets. All that is certain is that a divine per-
   sonage is addressed.

2b. I follow the editors in assuming that these lines,
   here numbered 2b, do not belong with those
   preceding them.

4. The geography in this poem is best understood
   if we observe that Catullus relates his itinerary
   backward, from Lake Garda, down the Po
   Valley, through the Adriatic, around Greece,
   across to Rhodes, through the Aegean Islands,
   through the Sea of Marmora (*Propontis*), and
   into the Black Sea to his starting point,
   Amastris, in Bithynia, some 200 miles east
   of the Bosphorus along the southern shore of
   the Black Sea.

7. *Cyrene:* a Greek city on the coast of Libya, center
   of the trade in asafoetida or sylphium, an

herb much used as a flavoring medium in ancient cookery.

Jove's hot temple: the shrine of Jupiter-Ammon on an oasis in the middle of the Sahara Desert.

Old Battus: traditional founder of Cyrene.

11. The geography of the first three strophes of this poem takes us to the Romans' "ends-of-the-world." Catullus starts with India, the farthest point in the East, then brings us back toward the West, through Hyrcania (southern end of the Caspian Sea) and Arabia; then he takes a jog to the northeast to Sacia (roughly comparable to the western part of Tibet), then southwest to Parthia (the northern part of Iran). From there he jumps south to Egypt, then northwestward to the Alps, the Rhineland, the English channel (the "fearsome sea"), and finally to Britain, last land of the West as India was last land of the East.

14. The point of this poem depends in part on the Roman custom of giving lawyers gifts of appreciation in lieu of money fees, the latter being forbidden by law. Calvus' client, a professor (his name is given as "Sulla" in the Latin), has given him an anthology of poetry, probably the only gift he could afford, since professors were as impecunious then as they are now. This Calvus sent to Catullus as a joke on the Saturnalia, the Roman winter festival that came at the end of December and in its gaiety and gift-giving corresponded to our Christmas season.

14b. A fragment. See note on 2b.

17. This poem is written in a sort of dance metre,

intended to suggest the folk dances of the Italian peasantry. It has a bouncy beat, full of humor and loud fun. The English version should be read with reminiscence of the dance hall, the minstrel show, or the burlesque pony chorus.

Jump Jim Crow: an anachronism, of course. The Latin is *sacra Salisubsili,* "rites of Salisubsilius." Nobody knows who "Salisubsilius" was —presumably a local deity whose rites were celebrated by dancing. His name means "Jump-jump-up," "Johnny-jump-up," or something of the sort.

18–20. There are no poems by these numbers in the manuscripts. We do not know whether they were lost, or whether the numbering as it stands represents the perpetuation of some early scribal error.

22. A note on the ancient book is perhaps appropriate here. It was made up of sheets of papyrus or parchment glued together to form a long, continuous strip, with the writing running cross-wise in narrow columns. The end of the strip was fastened to a stick, on each end of which were round knobs, or bosses; the whole long strip was tightly rolled around the stick and tied up with thongs, or laces, to prevent its unrolling. The edges of the roll were trimmed with a knife and rubbed smooth with pumice.

23. This poem is best understood as a parody of the Stoic paradox "that only the wise man is happy." Popular bowdlerization of Stoicism identified the "wise man" with the "poor man," and it is on this bit of pseudo philosophy that Catullus' poem rests. We should add, perhaps,

that to the Roman, "dryness of body"—absence of excessive "humors" in the system— was a sign of good health.

27. At Roman drinking bouts, one of the company was chosen *magister bibendi* "toastmaster," and directed the drinking of the group. The Romans, perhaps for reasons of economy, certainly not for those of sobriety, regularly diluted their wine with water. This was always done in proportions of three, as three parts of wine and six of water, six of wine and three of water, and so on as the *magister bibendi* might order. In this poem the party has reached the ultimate, for the guests are to drink their wine "straight" (*merum*). More than that, the *magister bibendi* is a woman, Postumia. This is highly unconventional, to say the least. Cicero would have been shocked. Nobody knows who Postumia was; if, as her august-sounding name suggests, she was a Roman lady, and not a slave or freedwoman, Cicero would have been doubly shocked. She should not even have been present.

29. The *Mamurra* of this poem was Julius Caesar's chief of engineers (*praefectus fabrum*) in Gaul. Catullus refers to him both by his proper name and by the pseudonym of *Mentula*. This latter I have ventured to translate, since without some English equivalent for it, most of the point of Catullus' lampoons against him would be lost. It means "Dickie-boy." For the rationale behind the translation, the reader is referred (*a*) to Harper's *Latin Dictionary* *s.v. mentula,* and (*b*) to the back-of-the-barn English of his youth.

The "father and son-in-law" referred to in

the last line are Caesar and Pompey. Pompey had married Caesar's daughter, Julia, as a result of one of many attempts made to patch up the increasing enmity between the two.

34. Roman paganism was extremely literalistic and legalistic; a prayer to a pagan deity required, to be effective, all of the precision of a legal document. In this hymn to Diana, Catullus preserves the canonical parts of the prayer, but relaxes the diction in the interests of poetry. The worshippers identify themselves and the deity herself, giving her pedigree, her main functions, then her subsidiary functions, together with the names appropriate to them, coming down finally to the particular function (in this case, goddess of agriculture) in virtue of which this prayer is addressed to her. Next a sort of saving clause is added, in which she is asked to consider as said any other name or function which she might happen to be fancying at the moment but which has been omitted by the worshippers. At the very end comes the petition itself: "Grant the blessing of thy saving goodness."

35. *"Our Lady of Dindymus":* Cybele. See introductory note to 63.

36. This poem contains a parody of the prayer form, on which see the note on 34. The places named were all famous for their temples of Venus (Aphrodite).

   The limping-footed god: Vulcan, god of fire.

37. *Boys with the liberty-caps:* Castor and Pollux, who were commonly represented wearing the *pilleus,* an ancient ancestor of the "liberty-cap" made famous by the French Revolution.

44. The point of the opening lines of this poem will

be abundantly clear if we realize that in Catullus' times Tibur (modern Tivoli) was a fashionable summer resort while the adjacent Sabine Hills were plain farmland. Catullus' villa must have been in a new development lying somewhere between the two.

51, 51b. These two poems appear as a single poem in the manuscripts. The first three strophes are Catullus' free version of part of Sappho's φαίνεταί μοι κῆνος ἶσος θέοισιν (the Greek text with an authoritative English translation is most readily available in D. L. Page, *Sappho and Alcaeus*, Oxford [1955], pp. 19–20); the final strophe (51b) has no connection whatever with Sappho's ode and seems to have no very obvious connection with Catullus' first three strophes either. Many scholars and some poets (including Walter Savage Landor) have believed that the fourth strophe is a fragment of another poem that came to be attached to the first three by a palaeographic or mechanical accident. Many other scholars and some other poets are equally convinced that the fourth strophe is an integral part of the whole poem and that the first three strophes are quite unprofitable without it. To this kind of philological and critical argument there is no foreseeable end and certainly no immediate solution. As my numbering shows, I have chosen to regard the fourth strophe as a separate fragment, but I am quite without any final conviction that I was right in so doing.

54. This is a conglomeration of fragments. The sentiment of the last two lines suggests that they

may be bits and scraps of a lampoon directed against Julius Caesar.

55. This poem, at least in my opinion, involves a bilingual pun on *Camerius,* a man's name, and καμάριον (*camarion*), a vulgar Greek word for the sash or "girdle" worn by Greek and Roman women partly as a waistband and partly as a support for the breasts. Catullus asks if "Camerius" (strictly speaking *Camerium,* since the name appears in the accusative case) "is here"; the girl replies by pulling back her dress and saying that her *camarion* "is here—but it'll take Hercules to get it!" The profession of the girl, and the significance of "getting her girdle" will, I think, be fairly obvious; I trust that my English-French pun "Jimmy's—chemise" is at least no worse than Catullus' Latin-Greek one.

56. Generations of scholars have wondered what it was that Cato (presumably Valerius Cato) was bound to find so funny. What the little boy was doing and what Catullus did to him are as vague in Catullus' gutter-Latin as they are in this somewhat prim English version. Something suggests itself, of course, but it seems at best only mildly amusing, like a mediocre dirty joke. Catullus is sometimes obscene, but rarely so dull. Probably we are missing the point.

58b. There is no argument here, as there is at 51b, about the connection of these lines with 58 preceding: they cannot possibly belong together, in spite of their being so written in the manuscripts.

61. *The Wedding Song of Vinia Aurunculeia and*

Manlius Torquatus. The song begins with an invocation of the god of weddings, Hymen (1–75). He is called from his home on Mount Helicon to join the wedding party, and in his curious role of both bride and groom is imagined as wearing the flower garland and scarlet veil of the bride, and her yellow sandals, and as carrying the torch of the husband, symbolic of the primitive custom of stealing the bride by night.

The second part of the song follows the procession of the bride from her home to that of her husband (76–155). A group of young boys, carrying torches, assemble at the bride's door, and call her out. After an appropriate show of reluctance, she comes; as she goes through the streets, the boys sing first of the joys of marriage and then take up the "Fescennine verses," a form of coarse banter, the purpose of which is to embarrass the bride and thus prevent her from being too happy: excessive joy might excite the jealousy of the gods. As the boys sing, they toss walnuts among the crowd as a symbol of fertility.

In its final section (156–end) the bride is received into her husband's house, and there formally put to bed by the matrons of honor. The husband is then called to go in to her, and the song ends with a wish that the couple may soon have children.

Some miscellaneous notes:

l. 18: *the Phrygian judge:* Paris.

l. 128, *et pass.:* "Pretty-boy" (Latin *concubinus*) is the young slave who up to now has been his master's favorite. There is no way to tell whether the homosexuality here implied was real or merely part of the convention of the Fescennines. In any event, it is included solely for the purpose of embarrassing the bride.

The lacunae indicated lines 79–85 and 112–14 are posited by the editors. In the manuscripts the text is continuous, but the lines as they stand do not make sense and are metrically inaccurate. Because of the strict metrical form in which the poem is written it is possible to determine the number of lines that have been lost and also to determine that line 85 and line 115 must be the last lines in their respective strophes. The placing of the remaining lines (lines 81, 83, and 111, in the present text) is conjectural.

62. *Vesper-Hesper:* The first is the Latin, the second the Greek name for the evening star. At lines 33–35, Hesper is said to return "with other name": his "other name" is *Eous,* the dawn star. Popular astronomy thought of the two as identical.

The lacuna between lines 32 and 33 is posited by the editors to account for the fact that the two lines, which in the manuscripts follow each other without interruption, do not belong together either in sense or in syntax. How many lines are lost we do not know. The poem is divided into sections, something like stanzas, which in most instances occur in pairs of equal length. On the supposition that there was originally such a pair of "stanzas" here, and on the conjecture that only the first line of the second "stanza" is missing, editors have presumed that seven lines have been lost. Of these they can supply with certainty only

the refrain ("O Hymen, wedding god," etc.),
which should have occurred at the end of the
first "stanza" as it does at the end of the
second.

63. *The Story of Attis.* This is Catullus' contribution
to the literature surrounding Cybele, the
Great Mother of the gods. Cybele, an Asiatic
goddess, the seat of whose worship was near
Mount Dindymus in Phrygia, was early identified with Rhea, sister and wife of Kronos, and
by him mother of the chief deities of the
Greek pantheon, Zeus, Hera, Hades (Pluto),
Poseidon, Hestia, and Demeter. Cybele's cult
statue was a natural stone, probably a me-
teorite, which was seized and transported to
Rome in 204 B.C. in response to an oracle
which had declared that only if this were
done could Hannibal be driven from Italy.
Her worship was conducted by eunuch priests,
called *Galli* or *Gallae,* and was wildly orgiastic
in character, accompanied by singing, dancing,
and the music of flute, cymbals, drums, trum-
pets, and gongs. Attis is her consort or chief
priest. By tradition he was a young man of
Athens who in a fit of religious frenzy fled
to Phrygia, castrated himself, and became
Cybele's devotee. It is this story that forms
the basis of Catullus' poem.

Some miscellaneous notes:

l. 10: *bull's-back: terga tauri,* a euphuism
for "drumhead."

ll. 42–43: "the Lord Sleep" is a god; Pasithea
is his consort.

ll. 65–67: A reference to boy-love. Attis' door
had been garlanded by his lovers.

l. 76: *lions:* Cybele is regularly represented
as riding in a chariot drawn by lions.

l. *77: ox-enemy: pecoris hostem,* a euphuism
for "lion."

64. This "little epic," usually called the "Peleus and
Thetis," actually contains two stories, one
inside the other. In brief outline, they are as
follows:

A. *The Marriage of Peleus and Thetis.*
Jupiter had become enamored of Thetis, one
of the daughters of Nereus, a sea god, but
having been warned by a prophecy that
Thetis' son would be greater than his father,
he decreed that Thetis must marry a mortal.
The standard versions of the myth have her
married against her will to Peleus, king of
Thessaly, but Catullus gives us instead a ro-
mantic tale of love at first sight. Peleus had
sailed with Jason and the Argonauts on the
quest of the golden fleece; as the Argo, the
first ship ever to sail the seas, passed on her
course, the Nereids rose up out of the waters
to see this strange new thing. Peleus caught
sight of Thetis, and she of him; instantly
they fell in love, and were subsequently married at Peleus' home, Pharsalus, in a gay
ceremony attended by both gods and men.
Their wedding-song, sung by the Fates (*Par-
cae*), foretold the birth of their great son,
Achilles.

B. *The Elopement of Theseus and Ariadne.*
Androgeos, son of King Minos of Crete, had
participated in the first celebration of athletic
games at Athens, and had defeated all his
adversaries in the wrestling contest. In a fit
of jealousy, Aegeus, king of Athens, had him
put to death. As a penalty, King Minos required the Athenians to send to Crete each
year seven young men and seven young

women, the finest in the city, to be fed to
the Minotaur. This creature, half man and
half bull, was the son of Minos' wife, Pasiphae,
by a bull, and was kept in the Labyrinth, a
maze from which escape was impossible.
Theseus, son of Aegeus, determined to put
an end to this slaughter by killing the Minotaur. He sailed from Athens with the other
young men and women in a ship carrying
a dark sail in sign of mourning. Arrived in
Crete, he found assistance in his venture from
Ariadne, daughter of Minos and Pasiphae,
who had fallen in love with him. Together
they devised the scheme by which Theseus
was to unwind a ball of yarn as he went into
the Labyrinth, thus providing him with a
method of finding his way out if he should
succeed in killing the Minotaur. Theseus
dispatched the monster, escaped from the
Labyrinth, and fled from Crete with Ariadne.
He spent his first night with her on the island
of Dia. In the morning he sailed away without her—forgot her, as the story goes. Ariadne
awoke, discovered her plight, and cursed
Theseus, praying that the state of mind which
had caused him to desert her might bring to
him a sorrow and despair comparable to her
own. Her prayer was answered, for Theseus
forgot to change the sail of his vessel from
dark to white, as he had been instructed to
do if he should succeed in killing the Minotaur; Aegeus, seeing the dark sail approach-
ing, thought that Theseus had been killed,
and in a frenzy of sorrow, threw himself into
the sea. Ariadne herself was rescued from Dia
by the god Dionysus (Bacchus) who made her
his wife.

Some miscellaneous notes:

l. 8: *The goddess of forts on city heights:* Athena.

l. 75: *a king unjust:* Minos, ordinarily famed for his justice.

l. 211: *Erechtheus:* a mythical king of Athens.

l. 227: *Spanish rust:* a dye giving presumably a dark purple or blue-black color.

l. 228: *Itonus' holy maid:* Athena.

ll. 290–91: *gentle sister of Phaethon:* the poplar tree.

l. 300: *your twin:* Diana.

l. 324: *Emathia:* Thessaly.

l. 346: *Pelops the Perjuror's third-in-line:* Agamemnon.

l. 367: *bonds of Neptune:* the walls of Troy, built by Neptune.

ll. 376–77: Thickening of the neck was popularly supposed to be a sign of lost virginity.

l. 387: *the Father:* Jupiter.

l. 390: *Liber:* Bacchus.

l. 391: *Thyiads:* Maenads.

l. 394: *Mavors:* Mars.

l. 395: *Lady of Triton:* Athena. *Rhamnus' maid:* Nemesis.

65. l. 2: *Learned Maids:* the Muses.

l. 9: The metre shows that at least one line has been lost here.

l. 14: *Daulias:* Philomela.

l. 16: *Callimachus:* See introductory note to 66.

66. This is Catullus' Latin version of a poem, "The Lock of Berenice," by the great scholar poet of Alexandria, Callimachus (*c.* 310–*c.* 240 B.C.). For the incident on which the poem is based, I can do no better than to quote E. T. Mer-

rill's introductory note: "Berenice, daughter of Magas, king of Cyrene, and wife of her cousin Ptolemy Euergetes (reigned 247–222 B.C.), king of Egypt, had for her husband's safety vowed to the gods a lock of her hair, when, shortly after his accession to the throne and marriage, the king was setting out on an expedition against Syria. Upon his safe return the vow was paid, and the tress deposited in the temple of the deified Arsinoë on the promontory of Zephyrion. Next morning, however, it had disappeared; but the anger of the king was appeased by the court astronomer, Conon, who said that he had descried it among the stars, where it must have been placed by divine agency. To verify his words Conon pointed out the hitherto undistinguished minor constellation which is now known as *Coma Berenices*."

Some miscellaneous notes:

ll. 43–46: The reference is to the promontory of Athos, through which Xerxes, king of Persia, cut a canal in the course of his campaign against Greece (480 B.C.). The poets persist in pretending that the canal was cut through Mount Athos itself, rather than through the narrow strip of land that separates the mainland from the promontory, at the outer end of which the mountain stands.

l. 44: *child of Thia:* the Sun.

l. 48: *Chalybian race:* the Chalybes, supposed inventors of the art of smelting iron.

ll. 52–54: This is a very vexed passage, and no satisfactory explanation of it has yet been found. We do not know to what story, or stories, Catullus is referring; in addition the

Latin text of line 54, which may contain the answer to the problem, is hopelessly corrupt. Memnon was a mythical king of Aethiopia, and was sometimes identified with a species of hawk. His *unigena,* which I have translated "twin," but which ought more properly to be translated "only child," remains a puzzle. Memnon had a twin brother, Emathion; of an "only child" we hear nothing. Since Arsinoë was represented as riding on an ostrich, it may be that this "twin" or "only child" was identified with that bird. The expression *ales equus,* "winged steed," may appear to bear this out, but even this much of the Latin text is not certain.

l. 57: *our Lady of Zephyris:* the deified Arsinoë, worshipped with the attributes of Aphrodite in a temple on the promontory of Zephyrion, about one hundred miles west of Alexandria.

l. 58: *Canopic:* Egyptian.

l. 59: The first half of this line is corrupt. No satisfactory emendation has as yet been proposed.

l. 60: *the golden crown from Ariadne's brow:* the wedding crown of Ariadne, placed by her husband, Dionysus, in the heavens.

ll. 65–68: This astronomical passage, with the names of various constellations, places the *Coma Berenices* between Virgo and Boötes ("the Herd"), near Leo and Ursa Major ("Callisto"). The Coma moves from east to west and sets before Boötes (hence "slow lags the Herd behind," etc.).

l. 70: *Tethys:* here stands for *Ocean.*

ll. 77–78: The Latin text here is confused and

has never been satisfactorily interpreted.

l. 94: *so might Orion beside Aquarius shine:*
that is, "even though the natural order should
be reversed." Orion is half way across the
heavens from Aquarius.

67. This is a gutter song, telling a particularly mal-
odorous version of an ancient and familiar
tale. Probably it should be regarded as an
experiment, to see how well a dignified poetic
form, the elegy, could be used as the vehicle
for obscenity, and conversely to see with what
success the coarsest of popular speech could
be made to produce poetry.

Miscellaneous notes:

l. 5: *son:* The Latin text is disputed here.
With Kroll, and others, I have adopted the
reading *nato,* originally proposed by Fröhlich.

l. 12: the Latin text of this line is badly
garbled. My version represents only what I
think the line might mean.

l. 32: *Brixia:* modern Brescia, about forty
miles west of Verona. *Tower Hill:* The translation again represents my guess at the meaning of a disputed Latin text.

68. Some scholars wish to divide this poem into two
or even more poems; others are equally certain that it is only one poem, or at most
two poems that were meant to be read together. There is, indeed, a clear-cut division
at line 40: the lines preceding it are addressed
to a "Manlius," the lines following it to an
"Allius," and there are other differences in
spirit, sentiment, and language between the
two. This is another one of those philological
problems to which no final solution will ever
be found. If we dismiss the matter of the dif-

ference in names—and it is probably less important than it seems—the poem can be read either as one rather rambling and discursive unit or as a "poetic package," with pt. I acting as an introduction to pt. II, much as 65 acts with respect to 66. If we prefer to think of it as two entirely separate poems, we can read lines 1–40 with entire satisfaction as one poem, and lines 41–160 as quite another, with equal satisfaction.

Some miscellaneous notes:

l. 47: At this point, as the metre shows, at least one line of the Latin text has been lost.

l. 53: *Aetna:* the volcano.

l. 54: *Malic springs of Oeta's Thermopylae:* Mount Oeta and the hot springs of Thermopylae lie reasonably close to each other near the district of Malis (Melis) in southeastern Thessaly.

l. 74: *Protesilaus and Laodamia:* Protesilaus and Laodamia were married just before Protesilaus set sail with the Greeks for Troy. In their haste they neglected to make appropriate sacrifices to the gods; their marriage thus remained unsanctified, and in retribution the gods caused Protesilaus to be the first Greek to fall at Troy.

ll. 109–117: Here is a poetic pudding of tales about Hercules, "He . . . whom fame falsefathers on Amphitryon" (that is, he who was reputed to be son of Amphitryon but was in fact the son of Zeus). Catullus compares the depth of Laodamia's passion to that of a canal, credited by the ancients to Hercules, that drained a swamp near the town of Pheneus and Mount Cyllene in Arcadia. With typical poetic exaggeration, Catullus had Hercules dig the canal through Mount Cyllene itself (cf. on Mount Athos, 66. 43–46); he goes on in quasi-learned fashion to "date" the digging of the canal by placing it at the time when Hercules, as one of the labors imposed upon him by Eurystheus (a mere mortal, hence "a worser lord"), slaughtered the man-eating birds of Stymphalus, a swamp near Pheneus. This and his other labors he performed in the hope of attaining divine status, or, as Catullus puts it, of adding one more deity to the pantheon ("that o'er heaven's gate more feet divine might pass"), and of marriage with Hebe, the goddess of youth ("and Hebe keep not long her maidenhood"). ll. 119–124: As if to balance the Greek simile of Hercules, Catullus introduces a purely Roman simile. Under the *lex Voconia*, of 169 B.C., no woman could be named as heir to an estate of over 100,000 sesterces. The "aged sire" in Catullus' simile has no son, but only a daughter; he is therefore faced with the unpleasant prospect of either dying intestate or of naming some collateral relative as his heir. This relative Catullus styles "the selfish kinsman," "the vulture," presumably because of his greedy hope that the "aged sire" will continue to lack an heir in the direct line. But just in time, the daughter bears a son ("that late-born babe," etc.); he is promptly named heir to his grandfather's wealth, and the disappointed kinsman, "joyless now," withdraws from the field. Protesilaus, says Catullus, was as dear to

Laodamia as is such a grandson to his grand-father.

ll. 141ff.: line 141 appears to be the beginning of some comment of the poet on the comparison he has just made between Juno and Lesbia; line 142 has no connection with it syntactically or logically. We must follow the editors in either (a) deleting both lines as spurious or (b) positing a lacuna of unknown length between the two.

l. 157: The last half of this line is garbled; no satisfactory emendation of it has as yet been proposed.

79. *Lesbius:* If we are right about "Lesbia" being Clodia, then "Lesbius" is certainly her brother, Clodius, Cicero's arch-enemy. His full name was Publius Clodius Pulcher; Catullus here puns on "Pulcher," which means "handsome" or (like Greek καλός, of which it is the standard translation) "fine."

90. *Persia's filthy cult:* a reference to the Magi, who were popularly supposed to practice incest.

95. *Cinna:* Gaius Helvius Cinna, the poet. His "Zmyrna," reputedly his masterpiece, dealt with Adonis.

116. *Battus' son:* Callimachus. See introductory note to 66.

SELECTED ANN ARBOR PAPERBACKS

works of enduring merit

For a complete list of Ann Arbor Paperback titles write:
THE UNIVERSITY OF MICHIGAN PRESS / ANN ARBOR